AF303802

Joyce Marx Machiavelli Chesterton Emerson Austen
Abbott Hardy Montaigne Cooper Hugo Grimm
Defoe Melville Haggard Eliot
Stoker Carroll Christie Molière
Wilde Maupassant Byron Schiller
Garnett Einstein Fitzgerald Engels Smith Kafka Hall
Goethe Hawthorne Willis
Cotton Dostoyevsky
Baum Kipling Doyle
Henry Nietzsche
Leslie Dumas Flaubert Turgenev Balzac
Stockton Vatsyayana Crane
Burroughs Verne
Curtis Tocqueville Gogol Vinci
Homer Widger Tolstoy Whitman Busch
Darwin Thoreau Twain
Potter Freud Zola Lawrence Scott Plato Harte
Kant Jowett Stevenson Dickens Hesse
Andersen Burton
London Descartes Cervantes Voltaire
Poe Aristotle Wells Cooke
Hale James Hastings Irving
Bunner Shakespeare
Richter Chambers
Doré Dante Chekhov da Shaw Benedict Alcott
Swift Pushkin Wodehouse
Newton

 tredition®

tredition was established in 2006 by Sandra Latusseck and Soenke Schulz. Based in Hamburg, Germany, tredition offers publishing solutions to authors and publishing houses, combined with world-wide distribution of printed and digital book content. tredition is uniquely positioned to enable authors and publishing houses to create books on their own terms and without conventional manu-facturing risks.

For more information please visit: www.tredition.com

TREDITION CLASSICS

This book is part of the TREDITION CLASSICS series. The creators of this series are united by passion for literature and driven by the intention of making all public domain books available in printed format again - worldwide. Most TREDITION CLASSICS titles have been out of print and off the bookstore shelves for decades. At tredi-tion we believe that a great book never goes out of style and that its value is eternal. Several mostly non-profit literature projects pro-vide content to tredition. To support their good work, tredition donates a portion of the proceeds from each sold copy. As a reader of a TREDITION CLASSICS book, you support our mission to save many of the amazing works of world literature from oblivion. See all available books at www.tredition.com.

Project Gutenberg

The content for this book has been graciously provided by Project Gutenberg. Project Gutenberg is a non-profit organization founded by Michael Hart in 1971 at the University of Illinois. The mission of Project Gutenberg is simple: To encourage the creation and distribu-tion of eBooks. Project Gutenberg is the first and largest collection of public domain eBooks.

Marse Henry - An Autobiography

Volume 1

Henry Watterson

Imprint

This book is part of TREDITION CLASSICS

Author: Henry Watterson
Cover design: Buchgut, Berlin – Germany

Publisher: tredition GmbH, Hamburg - Germany
ISBN: 978-3-8424-3363-2

www.tredition.com
www.tredition.de

"Marse Henry"

An Autobiography

By

Henry Watterson

Volume I

**TO MY FRIEND ALEXANDER KONTA WITH AFFECTIONATE
SALUTATION**

"Mansfield," 1919

A mound of earth a little higher graded:
Perhaps upon a stone a chiselled name:
A dab of printer's ink soon blurred and faded—
And then oblivion—that—that is fame!

—HENRY WATTERSON

Contents

Chapter the First

I Am Born and Begin to Take Notice—John Quincy Adams and Andrew
Jackson—James K. Polk and Franklin Pierce—Jack Dade and "Beau
Hickman"—Old Times in Washington

Chapter the Second

Slavery the Trouble-Maker—Break-Up of the Whig Party and Rise of the
Republican—The Key—Sickle's Tragedy—Brooks and Sumner—Life at
Washington in the Fifties

Chapter the Third

The Inauguration of Lincoln—I Quit Washington and Return to
Tennessee—A Run-a-bout with Forest—Through the Federal Lines and a
Dangerous Adventure—Good Luck at Memphis

Chapter the Fourth

I Go to London—Am Introduced to a Notable Set—
Huxley, Spencer, Mill and Tyndall—Artemus Ward
Comes to Town—The Savage Club

Chapter the Fifth

Mark Twain—The Original of Colonel Mulberry Sellers—The "Earl of
Durham"—Some Noctes Ambrosianæ—A Joke on Murat Halstead

Chapter the Sixth

Houston and Wigfall of Texas—Stephen A. Douglas—The Twaddle about
Puritans and Cavaliers—Andrew Johnson and John C. Breckenridge

Chapter the Seventh

An Old Newspaper Rookery — Reactionary Sectionalism in Cincinnati and
Louisville — *The Courier-Journal*

Chapter the Eighth

Feminism and Woman Suffrage — The Adventures in Politics and Society — A
Real Heroine

Chapter the Ninth

Dr. Norvin Green — Joseph Pulitzer — Chester A. Arthur — General
Grant — The Case of Fitz-John Porter

Chapter the Tenth

Of Liars and Lying — Woman Suffrage and Feminism — The Professional
Female — Parties, Politics, and Politicians in America

Chapter the Eleventh

Andrew Johnson — The Liberal Convention in 1872 — Carl Schurz — The
"Quadrilateral" — Sam Bowles, Horace White and Murat Halstead — A
Queer Composite of Incongruities

Chapter the Twelfth

The Ideal in Public Life — Politicians, Statesmen and Philosophers —
The Disputed Presidency in 1876 — The Persona and Character of Mr.

Tilden—His Election and Exclusion by a Partisan Tribunal

Illustrations

Henry Watterson (About 1908)

Henry Clay—Painted at Ashland by Dodge for The Hon. Andrew Ewing of
Tennessee-The Original Hangs in Mr. Watterson's Library at "Mansfield"

W. P. Hardee, Lieutenant General C.S.A.

John Bell of Tennessee—In 1860 Presidential Candidate "Union Party"—"Bell and Everett" Ticket

Artemus Ward

General Leonidas Polk—Lieutenant General C.S.A. Killed in Georgia, June 14, 1864—P. E. Bishop of Louisiana

Mr. Watterson's Editorial Staff in 1868 When the Three Daily Newspapers of Louisville Were United into the *Courier-Journal*. Mr. George D. Prentice and Mr. Watterson Are in the Center

Abraham Lincoln in 1861. From a Photograph by M. B. Brady

Mrs. Lincoln in 1861

"MARSE HENRY"

Chapter the First

I Am Born and Begin to Take Notice—John Quincy Adams and Andrew
Jackson—James K. Polk and Franklin Pierce—Jack Dade and "Beau
Hickman"—Old Times in Washington

I

I am asked to jot down a few autobiographic odds and ends from such data of record and memory as I may retain. I have been something of a student of life; an observer of men and women and affairs; an appraiser of their character, their conduct, and, on occasion, of their motives. Thus, a kind of instinct, which bred a tendency and grew to a habit, has led me into many and diverse companies, the lowest not always the meanest.

Circumstance has rather favored than hindered this bent. I was born in a party camp and grew to manhood on a political battlefield. I have lived through stirring times and in the thick of events. In a vein colloquial and reminiscential, not ambitious, let me recall some impressions which these have left upon the mind of one who long ago reached and turned the corner of the Scriptural limitation; who, approaching fourscore, does not yet feel painfully the frost of age beneath the ravage of time's defacing waves. Assuredly they have not obliterated his sense either of vision or vista. Mindful of the adjuration of Burns,

Keep something to yourself,
Ye scarcely tell to ony,

I shall yet hold little in reserve, having no state secrets or mysteries of the soul to reveal.

It is not my purpose to be or to seem oracular. I shall not write after the manner of Rousseau, whose Confessions had been better honored in the breach than the observance, and in any event whose sincerity will bear question; nor have I tales to tell after the manner of Paul Barras, whose Memoirs have earned him an immortality of infamy. Neither shall I emulate the grandiose volubility and self-complacent posing of Metternich and Talleyrand, whose pretentious volumes rest for the most part unopened upon dusty shelves. I aspire to none of the honors of the historian. It shall be my aim as far as may be to avoid the garrulity of the raconteur and to restrain the exaggerations of the ego. But neither fear of the charge of self-exploitation nor the specter of a modesty oft too obtrusive to be real shall deter me from a proper freedom of narration, where, though in the main but a humble chronicler, I must needs appear upon the scene and speak of myself; for I at least have not always been a dummy and have sometimes in a way helped to make history.

In my early life—as it were, my salad days—I aspired to becoming what old Simon Cameron called "one of those damned literary fellows" and Thomas Carlyle less profanely described as "a leeterary celeebrity." But some malign fate always sat upon my ambitions in this regard. It was easy to become The National Gambler in Nast's cartoons, and yet easier The National Drunkard through the medium of the everlasting mint-julep joke; but the phantom of the laurel crown would never linger upon my fair young brow.

Though I wrote verses for the early issues of Harper's Weekly—happily no one can now prove them on me, for even at that jejune period I had the prudence to use an anonym—the Harpers, luckily for me, declined to publish a volume of my poems. I went to London, carrying with me "the great American novel." It was actually accepted by my ever too partial friend, Alexander Macmillan. But, rest his dear old soul, he died and his successors refused to see the transcendent merit of that performance, a view which my own maturing sense of belles-lettres values subsequently came to verify.

When George Harvey arrived at the front I "'ad 'opes." But, Lord, that cast-iron man had never any bookish bowels of compassion — or political either for the matter of that! — so that finally I gave up fiction and resigned myself to the humble category of the crushed tragi-comedians of literature, who inevitably drift into journalism.

Thus my destiny has been casual. A great man of letters quite thwarted, I became a newspaper reporter — a voluminous space writer for the press — now and again an editor and managing editor — until, when I was nearly thirty years of age, I hit the Kentucky trail and set up for a journalist. I did this, however, with a big "J," nursing for a while some faint ambitions of statesmanship — even office — but in the end discarding everything that might obstruct my entire freedom, for I came into the world an insurgent, or, as I have sometimes described myself in the Kentucky vernacular, "a free nigger and not a slave nigger."

II

Though born in a party camp and grown to manhood on a political battlefield my earlier years were most seriously influenced by the religious spirit of the times. We passed to and fro between Washington and the two family homesteads in Tennessee, which had cradled respectively my father and mother, Beech Grove in Bedford County, and Spring Hill in Maury County. Both my grandfathers were devout churchmen of the Presbyterian faith. My Grandfather Black, indeed, was the son of a Presbyterian clergyman, who lived, preached and died in Madison County, Kentucky. He was descended, I am assured, in a straight line from that David Black, of Edinburgh, who, as Burkle tells us, having declared in a sermon that Elizabeth of England was a harlot, and her cousin,

Mary Queen of Scots, little better, went to prison for it—all honor to his memory.

My Grandfather Watterson was a man of mark in his day. He was decidedly a constructive—the projector and in part the builder of an important railway line—an early friend and comrade of General Jackson, who was all too busy to take office, and, indeed, who throughout his life disdained the ephemeral honors of public life. The Wattersons had migrated directly from Virginia to Tennessee.

The two families were prosperous, even wealthy for those days, and my father had entered public life with plenty of money, and General Jackson for his sponsor. It was not, however, his ambitions or his career that interested me—that is, not until I was well into my teens—but the camp meetings and the revivalist preachers delivering the Word of God with more or less of ignorant yet often of very eloquent and convincing fervor.

The wave of the great Awakening of 1800 had not yet subsided. Bascom was still alive. I have heard him preach. The people were filled with thoughts of heaven and hell, of the immortality of the soul and the life everlasting, of the Redeemer and the Cross of Calvary. The camp ground witnessed an annual muster of the adjacent countryside. The revival was a religious hysteria lasting ten days or two weeks. The sermons were appeals to the emotions. The songs were the outpourings of the soul in ecstacy. There was no fanaticism of the death-dealing, proscriptive sort; nor any conscious cant; simplicity, childlike belief in future rewards and punishments, the orthodox Gospel the universal rule. There was a good deal of doughty controversy between the churches, as between the parties; but love of the Union and the Lord was the bedrock of every confession.

Inevitably an impressionable and imaginative mind opening to such sights and sounds as it emerged from infancy must have been deeply affected. Until I was twelve years old the enchantment of religion had complete possession of my understanding. With the loudest, I could sing all the hymns. Being early taught in music I began to transpose them into many sorts of rhythmic movement for the edification of my companions. Their words, aimed directly at the heart, sank, never to be forgotten, into my memory. To this day I can repeat the most of them—though not without a break of voice—

while too much dwelling upon them would stir me to a pitch of feeling which a life of activity in very different walks and ways and a certain self-control I have been always able to command would scarcely suffice to restrain.

The truth is that I retain the spiritual essentials I learned then and there. I never had the young man's period of disbelief. There has never been a time when if the Angel of Death had appeared upon the scene — no matter how festal — I would not have knelt with adoration and welcome; never a time on the battlefield or at sea when if the elements had opened to swallow me I would not have gone down shouting!

Sectarianism in time yielded to universalism. Theology came to seem to my mind more and more a weapon in the hands of Satan to embroil and divide the churches. I found in the Sermon on the Mount leading enough for my ethical guidance, in the life and death of the Man of Galilee inspiration enough to fulfill my heart's desire; and though I have read a great deal of modern inquiry — from Renan and Huxley through Newman and Döllinger, embracing debates before, during and after the English upheaval of the late fifties and the Ecumenical Council of 1870, including the various raids upon the Westminster Confession, especially the revision of the Bible, down to writers like Frederic Harrison and Doctor Campbell — I have found nothing to shake my childlike faith in the simple rescript of Christ and Him crucified.

III

From their admission into the Union, the States of Kentucky and Tennessee have held a relation to the politics of the country somewhat disproportioned to their population and wealth. As between the two parties from the Jacksonian era to the War of Sections, each was closely and hotly contested. If not the birthplace of what was called "stump oratory," in them that picturesque form of party warfare flourished most and lasted longest. The "barbecue" was at once a rustic feast and a forum of political debate. Especially notable was the presidential campaign of 1840, the year of my birth, "Tippecanoe and Tyler," for the Whig slogan—"Old Hickory" and "the battle of New Orleans," the Democratic rallying cry—Jackson and Clay, the adored party chieftains.

I grew up in the one State, and have passed the rest of my life in the other, cherishing for both a deep affection, and, maybe, overestimating their hold upon the public interest. Excepting General Jackson, who was a fighter and not a talker, their public men, with Henry Clay and Felix Grundy in the lead, were "stump orators." He who could not relate and impersonate an anecdote to illustrate and clinch his argument, nor "make the welkin ring" with the clarion tones of his voice, was politically good for nothing. James K. Polk and James C. Jones led the van of stump orators in Tennessee, Ben Hardin, John J. Crittenden and John C. Breckenridge in Kentucky. Tradition still has stories to tell of their exploits and prowess, their wit and eloquence, even their commonplace sayings and doings. They were marked men who never failed to captivate their audiences. The system of stump oratory had many advantages as a public force and was both edifying and educational. There were a few conspicuous writers for the press, such as Ritchie, Greeley and Prentice. But the day of personal journalism and newspaper influence came later.

I was born at Washington—February 16, 1840—"a bad year for Democrats," as my father used to say, adding: "I am afraid the boy will grow up to be a Whig."

In those primitive days there were only Whigs and Democrats. Men took their politics, as their liquor, "straight"; and this father of mine was an undoubting Democrat of the schools of Jefferson and Jackson. He had succeeded James K. Polk in Congress when the future President was elected governor of Tennessee; though when nominated he was little beyond the age required to qualify as a member of the House.

To the end of his long life he appeared to me the embodiment of wisdom, integrity and couarge. And so he was—a man of tremendous force of character, yet of surpassing sweetness of disposition; singularly disdainful of office, and indeed of preferment of every sort; a profuse maker and a prodigal spender of money; who, his needs and recognition assured, cared nothing at all for what he regarded as the costly glories of the little great men who rattled round in places often much too big for them.

Immediately succeeding Mr. Polk, and such a youth in appearance, he attracted instant attention. His father, my grandfather, allowed him a larger income than was good for him—seeing that the per diem then paid Congressmen was altogethr insufficient—and during the earlier days of his sojourn in the national capital he cut a wide swath; his principal yokemate in the pleasures and dissipations of those times being Franklin Pierce, at first a representative and then a senator from New Hampshire. Fortunately for both of them, they were whisked out of Washington by their families in 1843; my father into the diplomatic service and Mr. Pierce to the seclusion of his New England home. They kept in close touch, however, the one with the other, and ten years later, in 1853, were back again upon the scene of their rather conspicuous frivolity, Pierce as President of the United States, my father, who had preceded him a year or two, as editor of the Washnigton Union, the organ of the Administration.

When I was a boy the national capital was still rife with stories of their escapades. One that I recall had it that on a certain occasion returning from an excursion late at night my father missed his footing and fell into the canal that then divided the city, and that Pierce, after many fruitless efforts, unable to assist him to dry land, exclaimed, "Well, Harvey, I can't get you out, but I'll get in with you," suiting the action to the word. And there they were found and rescued by a party of passers, very well pleased with themselves.

My father's absence in South America extended over two years. My mother's health, maybe her aversion to a long overseas journey, kept her at home, and very soon he tired of life abroad without her and came back. A committee of citizens went on a steamer down the river to meet him, the wife and child along, of course, and the story was told that, seated on the paternal knee curiously observant of every detail, the brat suddenly exclaimed, "Ah ha, pa! Now you've got on your store clothes. But when ma gets you up at Beech Grove you'll have to lay off your broadcloth and put on your jeans, like I do."

Being an only child and often an invalid, I was a pet in the family and many tales were told of my infantile precocity. On one occasion I had a fight with a little colored boy of my own age and I need not say got the worst of it. My grandfather, who came up betimes and separated us, said, "he has blackened your eye and he shall black your boots," thereafter making me a deed to the lad. We grew up together in the greatest amity and in due time I gave him his freedom, and again to drop into the vernacular—"that was the only nigger I ever owned." I should add that in the "War of Sections" he fell in battle bravely fighting for the freedom of his race.

It is truth to say that I cannot recall the time when I was not passionately opposed to slavery, a crank on the subject of personal liberty, if I am a crank about anything.

IV

In those days a less attractive place than the city of Washington could hardly be imagined. It was scattered over an ill-paved and half-filled oblong extending east and west from the Capitol to the White House, and north and south from the line of the Maryland hills to the Potomac River. One does not wonder that the early Britishers, led by Tom Moore, made game of it, for it was both unpromising and unsightly.

Private carriages were not numerous. Hackney coaches had to be especially ordered. The only public conveyance was a rickety old omnibus which, making hourly trips, plied its lazy journey between the Navy Yard and Georgetown. There was a livery stable—Kimball's—having "stalls," as the sleeping apartments above came to be called, thus literally serving man and beast. These stalls often lodged very distinguished people. Kimball, the proprietor, a New Hampshire Democrat of imposing appearance, was one of the last Washingtonians to wear knee breeches and a ruffled shirt. He was a great admirer of my father and his place was a resort of my childhood.

One day in the early April of 1852 I was humped in a chair upon one side of the open entrance reading a book—Mr. Kimball seated on the other side reading a newspaper—when there came down the street a tall, greasy-looking person, who as he approached said: "Kimball, I have another letter here from Frank."

"Well, what does Frank say?"

Then the letter was produced, read and discussed.

It was all about the coming National Democratic Convention and its prospective nominee for President of the United States, "Frank" seeming to be a principal. To me it sounded very queer. But I took it all in, and as soon as I reached home I put it up to my father:

"How comes it," I asked, "that a big old loafer gets a letter from a candidate for President and talks it over with the keeper of a livery stable? What have such people to do with such things?"

My father said: "My son, Mr. Kimball is an estimable man. He has been an important and popular Democrat in New Hampshire. He is not without influence here. The Frank they talked about is Gen. Franklin Pierce, of New Hampshire, an old friend and neighbor of Mr. Kimball. General Pierce served in Congress with me and some of us are thinking that we may nominate him for President. The 'big old loafer,' as you call him, was Mr. John C. Rives, a most distinguished and influential Democrat indeed."

Three months later, when the event came to pass, I could tell all about Gen. Franklin Pierce. His nomination was no surprise to me, though to the country at large it was almost a shock. He had been nowhere seriously considered.

In illustration of this a funny incident recurs to me. At Nashville the night of the nomination a party of Whigs and Democrats had gathered in front of the principal hotel waiting for the arrival of the news, among the rest Sam Bugg and Chunky Towles, two local gamblers, both undoubting Democrats. At length Chunky Towles, worn out, went off to bed. The result was finally flashed over the wires. The crowd was nonplused. "Who the hell is Franklin Pierce?" passed from lip to lip.

Sam Bugg knew his political catechism well. He proceeded at length to tell all about Franklin Pierce, ending with the opinion that he was the man wanted and would be elected hands down, and he had a thousand dollars to bet on it.

Then he slipped away to tell his pal.

"Wake up, Chunky," he cried. "We got a candidate—Gen. Franklin Pierce, of
New Hampshire."

"Who the——"

"Chunky," says Sam. "I am ashamed of your ignorance. Gen. Franklin Pierce is the son of Gen. Benjamin Pierce, of Revolutionary fame. He has served in both houses of Congress. He declined a seat in Polk's Cabinet. He won distinction in the Mexican War. He is the very candidate we've been after."

"In that case," says Chunky, "I'll get up." When he reappeared Petway, the Whig leader of the gathering, who had been deriding the convention, the candidate and all things else Democratic, exclaimed:

"Here comes Chunky Towles. He's a good Democrat; and I'll bet ten to one he never heard of Franklin Pierce in his life before."

Chunky Towles was one of the handsomest men of his time. His strong suit was his unruffled composure and cool self-control. "Mr. Petway," says he, "you would lose your money, and I won't take advantage of any man's ignorance. Besides, I never gamble on a certainty. Gen. Franklin Pierce, sir, is a son of Gen. Benjamin Pierce of Revolutionary memory. He served in both houses of Congress, sir—refused a seat in Polk's Cabinet, sir—won distinction in the Mexican War, sir. He has been from the first my choice, and I've money to bet on his election."

Franklin Pierce had an only son, named Benny, after his grandfather, the Revolutionary hero. He was of my own age. I was planning the good time we were going to have in the White House when tidings came that he had been killed in a railway accident. It was a grievous blow, from which the stricken mother never recovered.

One of the most vivid memories and altogether the saddest episode of my childhood is that a few weeks later I was carried up to the Executive Mansion, which, all formality and marble, seemed cold enough for a mausoleum, where a lady in black took me in her arms and convulsively held me there, weeping as if her heart would break.

V

Sometimes a fancy, rather vague, comes to me of seeing the soldiers go off to the Mexican War and of making flags striped with pokeberry juice — somehow the name of the fruit was mingled with that of the President — though a visit quite a year before to The Hermitage, which adjoined the farm of an uncle, to see General Jackson is still uneffaced.

I remember it vividly. The old hero dandled me in his arms, saying "So this is Harvey's boy," I looking the while in vain for the "hickory," of which I had heard so much.

On the personal side history owes General Jackson reparation. His personality needs indeed complete reconstruction in the popular mind, which misconceives him a rough frontiersman having few or none of the social graces. In point of fact he came into the world a gentleman, a leader, a knight-errant who captivated women and dominated men.

I shared when a young man the common belief about him. But there is ample proof of the error of this. From middle age, though he ever liked a horse race, he was a regular if not a devout churchman. He did not swear at all, "by the Eternal" or any other oath. When he reached New Orleans in 1814 to take command of the army, Governor Claiborne gave him a dinner; and after he had gone Mrs. Claiborne, who knew European courts and society better than any other American woman, said to her husband: "Call that man a backwoodsman? He is the finest gentleman I ever met!"

There is another witness—Mr. Buchanan, afterward President—who tells how he took a distinguished English lady to the White House when Old Hickory was President; how he went up to the general's private apartment, where he found him in a ragged *robe-de-chambre*, smoking his pipe; how, when he intimated that the President might before coming down slick himself a bit, he received the half-laughing rebuke: "Buchanan, I once knew a man in Virginia who made himself independently rich by minding his own business"; how, when he did come down, he was *en règle*; and finally how, after a half hour of delightful talk, the English lady as they regained the street broke forth with enthusiasm, using almost the selfsame words of Mrs. Claiborne: "He is the finest gentleman I ever met in the whole course of my life."

VI

The Presidential campaign of 1848—and the concurrent return of the Mexican soldiers—seems but yesterday. We were in Nashville, where the camp fires of the two parties burned fiercely day and night, Tennessee a debatable, even a pivotal state. I was an enthusiastic politician on the Cass and Butler side, and was correspondingly disappointed when the election went against us for Taylor and Fillmore, though a little mollified when, on his way to Washington, General Taylor grasping his old comrade, my grandfather, by the hand, called him "Billy," and paternally stroked my curls.

Though the next winter we passed in Washington I never saw him in the White
House. He died in July, 1850, and was succeeded by Millard Fillmore. It is
common to speak of Old Rough and Ready as an ignoramus. I don't think this.
He may not have been very courtly, but he was a gentleman.

Later in life I came to know Millard Fillmore well and to esteem him highly. Once he told me that Daniel Webster had said to him:

"Fillmore, I like Clay—I like Clay very much—but he rides rough, sir; damned rough!"

I was fond of going to the Capitol and of playing amateur page in the House, of which my father had been a member and where he had many friends, though I was never officially a page. There was in particular a little old bald-headed gentleman who was good to me and would put his arm about me and stroll with me across the rotunda to the Library of Congress and get me books to read. I was not so young as not to know that he was an ex-President of the United States, and to realize the meaning of it. He had been the oldest member of the House when my father was the youngest. He was John Quincy Adams. By chance I was on the floor of the House when he fell in his place, and followed the excited and tearful throng when they bore him into the Speaker's Room, kneeling by the side of the sofa with an improvised fan and crying as if my heart would break.

One day in the spring of 1851 my father took me to a little hotel on Pennsylvania Avenue near the Capitol and into a stuffy room, where a snuffy old man wearing an ill-fitting wig was busying himself over a pile of documents. He turned about and was very hearty.

"Aha, you've brought the boy," said he.

And my father said: "My son, you wanted to see General Cass, and here he is."

My enthusiasm over the Cass and Butler campaign had not subsided.
Inevitably General Cass was to me the greatest of heroes. My father had
been and always remained his close friend. Later along we dwelt together at
Willard's Hotel, my mother a chaperon for Miss Belle Cass, afterward Madame
Von Limbourg, and I came into familiar intercourse with the family.

The general made me something of a pet and never ceased to be a hero to me. I still think he was one of the foremost statesmen of his time and treasure a birthday present he made me when I was just entering my teens.

The hour I passed with him that afternoon I shall never forget.

As we were about taking our leave my father said: "Well, my son, you have seen General Cass; what do you think of him?"

And the general patting me affectionately on the head laughingly said: "He thinks he has seen a pretty good-looking old fogy — that is what he thinks!"

VII

There flourished in the village life of Washington two old blokes — no other word can proprly describe them — Jack Dade, who signed himself "the Honorable John W. Dade, of Virginia;" and Beau Hickman, who hailed from nowhere and acquired the pseudonym through sheer impudence. In one way and another they lived by their wits, the one all dignity, the other all cheek. Hickman fell very early in his career of sponge and beggar, but Dade lived long and died in office — indeed, toward the close an office was actually created for him.

Dade had been a schoolmate of John Tyler — so intimate they were that at college they were called "the two Jacks" — and when the death of Harrison made Tyler President, the "off Jack," as he dubbed himself, went up to the White House and said: "Jack Tyler, you've had luck and I haven't. You must do something for me and do it quick. I'm hard up and I want an office."

"You old reprobate," said Tyler, "what office on earth do you think you are fit to fill?"

"Well," said Dade, "I have heard them talking round here of a place they call a sine-cu-ree — big pay and no work — and if there is one of them left and lying about loose I think I could fill it to a T."

"All right," said the President good naturedly, "I'll see what can be done.

Come up to-morrow."

The next day "Col. John W. Dade, of Virginia," was appointed keeper of the Federal prison of the District of Columbia. He assumed his post with *empressement*, called the prisoners before him and made them an address.

"Ladies and gentlemen," said he; "I have been chosen by my friend, the President of the United States, as superintendent of this eleemosynary institution. It is my intention to treat you all as a Virginia gentleman should treat a body of American ladies and gentlemen gathered here from all parts of our beloved Union, and I shall expect the same consideration in return. Otherwise I will turn you all out upon the cold mercies of a heartless world and you will have to work for your living."

There came to Congress from Alabama a roistering blade by the name of McConnell. He was something of a wit. During his brief sojourn in the national capital he made a noisy record for himself as an all-round, all-night man about town, a dare-devil and a spendthrift. His first encounter with Col. John W. Dade, of Virginia, used to be one of the standard local jokes. Colonel Dade was seated in the barroom of Brown's Hotel early one morning, waiting for someone to come in and invite him to drink.

Presently McConnell arrived. It was his custom when he entered a saloon to ask the entire roomful, no matter how many, "to come up and licker," and, of course, he invited the solitary stranger.

When the glasses were filled Dade pompously said: "With whom have I the honor of drinking?"

"My name," answered McConnell, "is Felix Grundy McConnell, begad! I am a member of Congress from Alabama. My mother is a justice of the peace, my aunt keeps a livery stable, and my grandmother commanded a company in the Revolution and fit the British, gol darn their souls!"

Dade pushed his glass aside.

"Sir," said he, "I am a man of high aspirations and peregrinations and can have nothing to do with such low-down scopangers as yourself. Good morning, sir!"

It may be presumed that both spoke in jest, because they became inseparable companions and the best of friends.

McConnell had a tragic ending. In James K. Polk's diary I find two entries under the dates, respectively, of September 8 and September 10, 1846. The first of these reads as follows: "Hon. Felix G. McConnell, a representative in Congress from Alabama called. He looked very badly and as though he had just recovered from a fit of intoxication. He was sober, but was pale, his countenance haggard and his system nervous. He applied to me to borrow one hundred dollars and said he would return it to me in ten days.

"Though I had no idea that he would do so I had a sympathy for him even in his dissipation. I had known him in his youth and had not the moral courage to refuse. I gave him the one hundred dollars in gold and took his note. His hand was so tremulous that he could scarcely write his name to the note legibly. I think it probable that he will never pay me. He informed me he was detained at Washington attending to some business in the Indian Office. I supposed he had returned home at the adjournment of Congress until he called to-day. I doubt whether he has any business in Washington, but fear he has been detained by dissipation."

The second of Mr. Polk's entries is a corollary of the first and reads: "About dark this evening I learned from Mr. Voorhies, who is acting as my private secretary during the absence of J. Knox Walker, that Hon. Felix G. McConnell, a representative in Congress from the state of Alabama, had committed suicide this afternoon at the St. Charles Hotel, where he boarded. On Tuesday last Mr. McConnell called on me and I loaned him one hundred dollars. [See this diary of that day.] I learn that but a short time before the horrid deed was committed he was in the barroom of the St. Charles Hotel handling gold pieces and stating that he had received them from me, and that he loaned thirty-five dollars of them to the barkeeper, that shortly afterward he had attempted to write something, but what I have not learned, but he had not written much when he said he would go to his room.

"In the course of the morning I learn he went into the city and paid a hackman a small amount which he owed him. He had locked his room door, and when found he was stretched out on his back with his hands extended, weltering in his blood. He had three wounds in the abdomen and his throat was cut. A hawkbill knife was found near him. A jury of inquest was held and found a verdict that he had destroyed himself. It was a melancholy instance of the effects of intemperance. Mr. McConnell when a youth resided at Fayetteville in my congressional district. Shortly after he grew up to manhood he was at my instance appointed postmaster of that town. He was a true Democrat and a sincere friend of mine.

"His family in Tennessee are highly respectable and quite numerous. The information as to the manner and particulars of his death I learned from Mr. Voorhies, who reported it to me as he had heard it in the streets. Mr. McConnell removed from Tennessee to Alabama some years ago, and I learn he has left a wife and three or four children."

Poor Felix Grundy McConnell! At a school in Tennessee he was a roommate of my father, who related that one night Felix awakened with a scream from a bad dream he had, the dream being that he had cut his own throat.

"Old Jack Dade," as he was always called, lived on, from hand to mouth, I dare say—for he lost his job as keeper of the district prison—yet never wholly out-at-heel, scrupulously neat in his person no matter how seedy the attire. On the completion of the new wings of the Capitol and the removal of the House to its more commodious quarters he was made custodian of the old Hall of Representatives, a post he held until he died.

VIII

Between the idiot and the man of sense, the lunatic and the man of genius, there are degrees—streaks—of idiocy and lunacy. How many expectant politicians elected to Congress have entered Washington all hope, eager to dare and do, to come away broken in health, fame and fortune, happy to get back home — sometimes unable to get away, to linger on in obscurity and poverty to a squalid and wretched old age.

I have lived long enough to have known many such: Senators who have filled the galleries when they rose to speak; House heroes living while they could on borrowed money, then hanging about the hotels begging for money to buy drink.

There was a famous statesman and orator who came to this at last, of whom the typical and characteristic story was told that the holder of a claim against the Government, who dared not approach so great a man with so much as the intimation of a bribe, undertook by argument to interest him in the merit of the case.

The great man listened and replied: "I have noticed you scattering your means round here pretty freely but you haven't said 'turkey' to me."

Surprised but glad and unabashed the claimant said "I was coming to that," produced a thousand-dollar bank roll and entered into an understanding as to what was to be done next day, when the bill was due on the calendar.

The great man took the money, repaired to a gambling house, had an extraordinary run of luck, won heavily, and playing all night, forgetting about his engagement, went to bed at daylight, not appearing in the House at all. The bill was called, and there being nobody to represent it, under the rule it went over and to the bottom of the calendar, killed for that session at least.

The day after the claimant met his recreant attorney on the avenue face to face and took him to task for his delinquency.

"Ah, yes," said the great man, "you are the little rascal who tried to bribe me the other day. Here is your dirty money. Take it and be off with you. I was just seeing how far you would go."

The comment made by those who best knew the great man was that if instead of winning in the gambling house he had lost he would have been up betimes at his place in the House, and doing his utmost to pass the claimant's bill and obtain a second fee.

Another memory of those days has to do with music. This was the coming of Jenny Lind to America. It seemed an event. When she reached Washington Mr. Barnum asked at the office of my father's newspaper for a smart lad to sell the programs of the concert—a new thing in artistic showmanry. "I don't want a paper carrier, or a newsboy," said he, "but a young gentleman, three or four young gentlemen." I was sent to him. We readily agreed upon the commission to be received—five cents on each twenty-five cent program—the oldest of old men do not forget such transactions. But, as an extra percentage for "organizing the force," I demanded a concert seat. Choice seats were going at a fabulous figure and Barnum at first demurred. But I told him I was a musical student, stood my ground, and, perhaps seeing something unusual in the eager spirit of a little boy, he gave in and the bargain was struck.

Two of my pals became my assistants. But my sales beat both of them hollow. Before the concert began I had sold my programs and was in my seat. I recall that my money profit was something over five dollars.

The bell-like tones of the Jenny Lind voice in "Home, Sweet Home," and "The Last Rose of Summer" still come back to me, but too long after for me to make, or imagine, comparisons between it and the vocalism of Grisi, Sontag and Parepa-Rosa.

Meeting Mr. Barnum at Madison Square Garden in New York, when he was running one of his entertainments there, I told him the story, and we had a hearty laugh, both of us very much pleased, he very much surprised to find in me a former employee.

One of my earliest yearnings was for a home. I cannot recall the time when I was not sick and tired of our migrations between Washington City and the two grand-paternal homesteads in Tennessee. The travel counted for much of my aversion to the nomadic life we led. The stage-coach is happier in the contemplation than in the actuality. Even when the railways arrived there were no sleeping cars, the time of transit three or four days and nights. In the earlier journeys it had been ten or twelve days.

Chapter the Second

Slavery the Trouble-Maker — Break-Up of the Whig Party and Rise of the
Republican — The Key — Sickle's Tragedy — Brooks and Sumner — Life at
Washington in the Fifties

I

Whether the War of Sections — as it should be called, because, except in Eastern Tennessee and in three of the Border States, Maryland, Kentucky and Missouri, it was nowise a civil war — could have been averted must ever remain a question of useless speculation. In recognizing the institution of African slavery, with no provision for its ultimate removal, the Federal Union set out embodying the seeds of certain trouble. The wiser heads of the Constitutional Convention perceived this plainly enough; its dissonance to the logic of their movement; on the sentimental side its repugnancy; on the practical side its doubtful economy; and but for the tobacco growers and the cotton planters it had gone by the board. The North soon found slave labor unprofitable and rid itself of slavery. Thus, restricted to the South, it came to represent in the Southern mind a "right" which the South was bound to defend.

Mr. Slidell told me in Paris that Louis Napoleon had once said to him in answer to his urgency for the recognition of the Southern Confederacy: "I have talked the matter over with Lord Palmerston and we are both of the opinion that as long as African slavery exists at the South, France and England cannot recognize the Confederacy. They do not demand its instant abolition. But if you put it in course of abatement and final abolishment through a term of years — I do not care how many—we can intervene to some purpose. As matters stand we dare not go before a European congress with such a proposition."

Mr. Slidell passed it up to Richmond. Mr. Davis passed it on to the generals in the field. The response he received on every hand was the statement that it would disorganize and disband the Confederate Armies. Yet we are told, and it is doubtless true, that scarcely one Confederate soldier in ten actually owned a slave.

Thus do imaginings become theories, and theories resolve themselves into claims; and interests, however mistaken, rise to the dignity of prerogatives.

II

The fathers had rather a hazy view of the future. I was witness to the decline and fall of the old Whig Party and the rise of the Republican Party. There was a brief lull in sectional excitement after the Compromise Measures of 1850, but the overwhelming defeat of the Whigs in 1852 and the dominancy of Mr. Jefferson Davis in the cabinet of Mr. Pierce brought the agitation back again. Mr. Davis was a follower of Mr. Calhoun—though it may be doubted whether Mr. Calhoun would ever have been willing to go to the length of secession—and Mr. Pierce being by temperament a Southerner as well as in opinions a pro-slavery Democrat, his Administration fell under the spell of the ultra Southern wing of the party. The Kansas-Nebraska Bill was originaly harmless enough, but the repeal of the Missouri Compromise, which on Mr. Davis' insistence was made a part of it, let slip the dogs of war.

In Stephen A. Douglas was found an able and pliant instrument. Like Clay,
Webster and Calhoun before him, Judge Douglas had the presidential bee in
his bonnet. He thought the South would, as it could, nominate and elect him

President.

Personally he was a most lovable man—rather too convivial—and for a while in 1852 it looked as though he might be the Democratic nominee. His candidacy was premature, his backers overconfident and indiscreet.

"I like Douglas and am for him," said Buck Stone, a member of Congress and delegate to the National Democratic Convention from Kentucky, "though I consider him a good deal of a damn fool." Pressed for a reason he continued; "Why, think of a man wanting to be President at forty years of age, and obliged to behave himself for the rest of his life! I wouldn't take the job on any such terms."

The proposed repeal of the Missouri Compromise opened up the slavery debate anew and gave it increased vitality. Hell literally broke loose among the political elements. The issues which had divided Whigs and Democrats went to the rear, while this one paramount issue took possession of the stage. It was welcomed by the extremists of both sections, a very godsend to the beaten politicians led by Mr. Seward. Rampant sectionalism was at first kept a little in the background. There were on either side concealments and reserves. Many patriotic men put the Union above slavery or antislavery. But the two sets of rival extremists had their will at last, and in seven short years deepened and embittered the contention to the degree that disunion and war seemed, certainly proved, the only way out of it.

The extravagance of the debates of those years amazes the modern reader. Occasionally when I have occasion to recur to them I am myself nonplussed, for they did not sound so terrible at the time. My father was a leader of the Union wing of the Democratic Party— headed in 1860 the Douglas presidential ticket in Tennessee—and remained a Unionist during the War of Sections. He broke away from Pierce and retired from the editorship of the Washiongton Union upon the issue of the repeal of the Missouri Compromise, to which he was opposed, refusing the appointment of Governor of Oregon, with which the President sought to placate him, though it meant his return to the Senate of the United States in a year or two, when he and Oregon's delegate in Congress, Gen. Joseph Lane—the

Lane of the Breckenridge and Lane ticket of 1860—had brought the territory of Oregon in as a state.

I have often thought just where I would have come in and what might have happened to me if he had accepted the appointment and I had grown to manhood on the Pacific Coast. As it was I attended a school in Philadelphia—the Protestant Episcopal Academy—came home to Tennessee in 1856, and after a season with private tutors found myself back in the national capital in 1858.

It was then that I began to nurse some ambitions of my own. I was going to be a great man of letters. I was going to write histories and dramas and romances and poetry. But as I had set up for myself I felt in honor bound meanwhile to earn my own living.

III

I take it that the early steps of every man to get a footing may be of interest when fairly told. I sought work in New York with indifferent success. Mr. Raymond of the Times, hearing me play the piano at which from childhood I had received careful instruction, gave me a job as "musical critic" during the absence of Mr. Seymour, the regular critic. I must have done my work acceptably, since I was not fired. It included a report of the debut of my boy-and-girl companion, Adelina Patti, when she made her first appearance in opera at the Academy of Music. But, as the saying is, I did not "catch on." There might be a more promising opening in Washington, and thither I repaired.

The Daily States had been established there by John P. Heiss, who with
Thomas Ritchie had years before established the Washington Union. Roger A.
Pryor was its nominal editor. But he soon took himself home to his beloved
Virginia and came to Congress, and the editorial writing on the States was

being done by Col. A. Dudley Mann, later along Confederate com-
missioner to
France, preceding Mr. Slidell.

Colonel Mann wished to work incognito. I was taken on as a kind
of go-between and, as I may say, figurehead, on the strength of
being my father's son and a very self-confident young gentleman,
and began to get my newspaper education in point of fact as a kind
of fetch-and-carry for Major Heiss. He was a practical newspaper
man who had started the Union at Nashville as well as the Union at
Washington and the Crescent—maybe it was the Delta—at New
Orleans; and for the rudiments of newspaper work I could scarcely
have had a better teacher.

Back of Colonel Mann as a leader writer on the States was a re-
markable woman. She was Mrs. Jane Casneau, the wife of Gen.
George Casneau, of Texas, who had a claim before Congress.
Though she was unknown to fame, Thomas A. Benton used to say
that she had more to do with making and ending the Mexican War
than anybody else.

Somewhere in the early thirties she had gone with her newly
wedded husband, an adventurous Yankee by the name of Storm, to
the Rio Grande and started a settlement they called Eagle Pass.
Storm died, the Texas outbreak began, and the young widow was
driven back to San Antonio, where she met and married Casneau,
one of Houston's lieutenants, like herself a New Yorker. She was
sent by Polk with Pillow and Trist to the City of Mexico and actually wrote the final treaty. It was she who dubbed William Walker
"the little gray-eyed man of destiny," and put the nickname "Old
Fuss and Feathers" on General Scott, whom she heartily disliked.

[Illustration: Henry Clay—Painted at Ashland by Dodge for the
Hon. Andrew
Ewing of Tennessee—The Original Hangs in Mr. Watterson's Li-
brary at
"Mansfield"]

A braver, more intellectual woman never lived. She must have
been a beauty in her youth; was still very comely at fifty; but a born

insurrecto and a terror with her pen. God made and equipped her for a filibuster. She possessed infinite knowledge of Spanish-American affairs, looked like a Spanish woman, and wrote and spoke the Spanish language fluently. Her obsession was the bringing of Central America into the Federal Union. But she was not without literary aspirations and had some literary friends. Among these was Mrs. Southworth, the novelist, who had a lovely home in Georgetown, and, whatever may be said of her works and articles, was a lovely woman. She used to take me to visit this lady. With Major Heiss she divided my newspaper education, her part of it being the writing part. Whatever I may have attained in that line I largely owe to her. She took great pains with me and mothered me in the absence of my own mother, who had long been her very dear friend. To get rid of her, or rather her pen, Mr. Buchanan gave General Casneau, when the Douglas schism was breaking out, a Central American mission, and she and he were lost by shipwreck on their way to this post, somewhere in Caribbean waters.

My immediate yokemate on the States was John Savage, "Jack," as he was commonly called; a brilliant Irishman, who with Devin Reilley and John Mitchel and Thomas Francis Meagher, his intimates, and Joseph Brennan, his brother-in-law, made a pretty good Irishman of me. They were '48 men, with literary gifts of one sort and another, who certainly helped me along with my writing, but, as matters fell out, did not go far enough to influence my character, for they were a wild lot, full of taking enthusiasm and juvenile decrepitude of judgment, ripe for adventures and ready for any enterprise that promised fun and fighting.

Between John Savage and Mrs. Casneau I had the constant spur of commendation and assistance as well as affection. I passed all my spare time in the Library of Congress and knew its arrangements at least as well as Mr. Meehan, the librarian, and Robert Kearon, the assistant, much to the surprise of Mr. Spofford, who in 1861 succeeded Mr. Meehan as librarian.

Not long after my return to Washington Col. John W. Forney picked me up, and I was employed in addition to my not very arduous duties on the States to write occasional letters from Washington to the Philadelphia Press. Good fortune like ill fortune rarely comes singly. Without anybody's interposition I was appointed to a clerkship, a real "sinecure," in the Interior Department by Jacob Thompson, the secretary, my father's old colleague in Congress. When the troubles of 1860-61 rose I was literally doing "a land-office business," with money galore and to spare. Somehow, I don't know how, I contrived to spend it, though I had no vices, and worked like a hired man upon my literary hopes and newspaper obligations.

Life in Washington under these conditions was delightful. I did not know how my heart was wrapped up in it until I had to part from it. My father stood high in public esteem. My mother was a leader in society. All doors were open to me. I had many friends. Going back to Tennessee in the midsummer of 1861, via Pittsburgh and Cincinnati, there happened a railway break and a halt of several hours at a village on the Ohio. I strolled down to the river and sat myself upon the brink, almost despairing—nigh heartbroken— when I began to feel an irresistible fascination about the swift-flowing stream. I leaped to my feet and ran away; and that is the only thought of suicide that I can recall.

IV

Mrs. Clay, of Alabama, in her "Belle of the Fifties" has given a graphic picture of life in the national capital during the administrations of Pierce and Buchanan. The South was very much in the saddle. Pierce, as I have said, was Southern in temperament, and Buchanan, who to those he did not like or approve had, as Arnold Harris said, "a winning way of making himself hateful," was an aristocrat under Southern and feminine influence.

I was fond of Mr. Pierce, but I could never endure Mr. Buchanan. His very voice gave offense to me. Directed by a periodical publication to make a sketch of him to accompany an engraving, I did my best on it.

Jacob Thompson, the Secretary of the Interior, said to me: "Now, Henry, here's your chance for a foreign appointment."

I now know that my writing was clumsy enough and my attempt to play the courtier clumsier still. Nevertheless, as a friend of my father and mother "Old Buck" might have been a little more considerate than he was with a lad trying to please and do him honor. I came away from the White House my *amour propre* wounded, and though I had not far to go went straight into the Douglas camp.

Taking nearly sixty years to think it over I have reached the conclusion that Mr. Buchanan was the victim of both personal and historic injustice. With secession in sight his one aim was to get out of the White House before the scrap began. He was of course on terms of intimacy with all the secession leaders, especially Mr. Slidell, of Louisiana, like himself a Northerner by birth, and Mr. Mason, a thick-skulled, ruffle-shirted Virginian. It was not in him or in Mr. Pierce, with their antecedents and associations, to be uncompromising Federalists. There was no clear law to go on. Moderate men were in a muck of doubt just what to do. With Horace Greeley Mr. Buchanan was ready to say "Let the erring sisters go." This indeed was the extent of Mr. Pierce's pacifism during the War of Sections.

A new party risen upon the remains of the Whig Party — the Republican Party — was at the door and coming into power. Lifelong pro-slavery Democrats could not look on with equanimity, still less with complaisance, and doubtless Pierce and Buchanan to the end of their days thought less of the Republicans than of the Confederates. As a consequence Republican writers have given quarter to neither of them.

It will not do to go too deeply into the account of those days. The times were out of joint. I knew of two Confederate generals who first tried for commissions in the Union Army; gallant and good fellows too; but they are both dead and their secret shall die with me. I knew likewise a famous Union general who was about to resign his commission in the army to go with the South but was prevented by his wife, a Northern woman, who had obtained of Mr. Lincoln a brigadier's commission.

V

In 1858 a wonderful affair came to pass. It was Mrs. Senator Gwin's fancy dress ball, written of, talked of, far and wide. I did not get to attend this. My costume was prepared—a Spanish cavalier, Mrs. Casneau's doing—when I fell ill and had with bitter disappointment to read about it next day in the papers. I was living at Willard's Hotel, and one of my volunteer nurses was Mrs. Daniel E. Sickles, a pretty young thing who was soon to become the victim of a murder and world scandal. Her husband was a member of the House from New York, and during his frequent absences I used to take her to dinner. Mr. Sickles had been Mr. Buchanan's Secretary of Legation in London, and both she and he were at home in the White House.

She was an innocent child. She never knew what she was doing, and when a year later Sickles, having killed her seducer—a handsome, unscrupulous fellow who understood how to take advantage of a husband's neglect—forgave her and brought her home in the face of much obloquy, in my heart of hearts I did homage to his courage and generosity, for she was then as he and I both knew a dying woman. She did die but a few months later. He was by no means a politician after my fancy or approval, but to the end of his days I was his friend and could never bring myself to join in the repeated public outcries against him.

Early in the fifties Willard's Hotel became a kind of headquarters for the two political extremes. During a long time their social intercourse was unrestrained—often joyous. They were too far apart, figuratively speaking, to come to blows. Truth to say, their aims were after all not so far apart. They played to one another's lead. Many a time have I seen Keitt, of South Carolina, and Burlingame, of Massachusetts, hobnob in the liveliest manner and most public places.

It is certainly true that Brooks was not himself when he attacked Sumner. The Northern radicals were wont to say, "Let the South go," the more profane among them interjecting "to hell!" The Secessionists liked to prod the New Englanders with what the South was going to do when they got to Boston. None of them really meant it—not even Toombs when he talked about calling the muster roll of his slaves beneath Bunker Hill Monument; nor Hammond, the son of a New England schoolmaster, when he spoke of the "mudsills of the North," meaning to illustrate what he was saying by the under-pinning of a house built on marshy ground, and not the Northern work people.

Toombs, who was a rich man, not quite impoverished by the war, banished himself in Europe for a number of years. At length he came home, and passing the White House at Washington he called and sent his card to the President. General Grant, the most genial and generous of men, had him come directly up.

[Illustration: W. P. Hardee, Lieutenant General C.S.A.]

"Mr. President," said Toombs, "in my European migrations I have made it a rule when arriving in a city to call first and pay my respects to the Chief of Police."

The result was a most agreeable hour and an invitation to dinner. Not long after this at the hospitable board of a Confederate general, then an American senator, Toombs began to prod Lamar about his speech in the House upon the occasion of the death of Charles Sumner. Lamar was not quick to quarrel, though when aroused a man of devilish temper and courage. The subject had become distasteful to him. He was growing obviously restive under Toombs' banter. The ladies of the household apprehending what was coming left the table.

Then Lamar broke forth. He put Toombs' visit to Grant, "crawling at the seat of power," against his eulogy of a dead enemy. I have never heard such a scoring from one man to another. It was magisterial in its dignity, deadly in its diction. Nothing short of a duel could have settled it in the olden time. But when Lamar, white with rage, had finished, Toombs without a ruffle said, "Lamar, you surprise me," and the host, with the rest of us, took it as a signal to rise from table and rejoin the ladies in the drawing-room. Of course nothing came of it.

Toombs was as much a humorist as an extremist. I have ridden with him under fire and heard him crack jokes with Minié balls flying uncomfortably about. Some one spoke kindly of him to old Ben Wade. "Yes, yes," said Wade; "I never did believe in the doctrine of total depravity."

But I am running ahead in advance of events.

VI

There came in 1853 to the Thirty-third Congress a youngish, dapper and graceful man notable as the only Democrat in the Massachusetts delegation. It was said that he had been a dancing master, his wife a work girl. They brought with them a baby in arms with the wife's sister for its nurse—a mis-step which was quickly corrected. I cannot now tell just how I came to be very intimate with them except that they lived at Willard's Hotel. His name had a pretty sound to it—Nathaniel Prentiss Banks.

A schoolmate of mine and myself, greatly to the mirth of those about us, undertook Mr. Banks' career. We were going to elect him Speaker of the next House and then President of the United States. This was particularly laughable to my mother and Mrs. Linn Boyd, the wife of the contemporary Speaker, who had very solid presidential aspirations of his own.

The suggestion perhaps originated with Mrs. Banks, to whom we two were ardently devoted. I have not seen her since those days, more than sixty years ago. But her beauty, which then charmed me, still lingers in my memory—a gentle, sweet creature who made much of us boys—and two years later when Mr. Banks was actually elected Speaker I was greatly elated and took some of the credit to myself. Twenty years afterwards General Banks and I had our seats close together in the Forty-fourth Congress, and he did not recall me at all or the episode of 1853. Nevertheless I warmed to him, and when during Cleveland's first term he came to me with a hard-luck story I was glad to throw myself into the breach. He had been a Speaker of the House, a general in the field and a Governor of Massachusetts, but was a faded old man, very commonplace, and except for the little post he held under Government pitiably helpless.

Colonel George Walton was one of my father's intimates and an imposing and familiar figure about Washington. He was the son of a signer of the Declaration of Independence, a distinction in those days, had been mayor of Mobile and was an unending raconteur. To my childish mind he appeared to know everything that ever had been or ever would be. He would tell me stories by the hour and send me to buy him lottery tickets. I afterward learned that that form of gambling was his mania. I also learned that many of his stories were apocryphal or very highly colored.

One of these stories especially took me. It related how when he was on a yachting cruise in the Gulf of Mexico the boat was over-hauled by pirates, and how he being the likeliest of the company was tied up and whipped to make him disgorge, or tell where the treasure was.

"Colonel Walton," said I, "did the whipping hurt you much?"

"Sir," he replied, as if I were a grown-up, "they whipped me until I was perfectly disgusted."

An old lady in Philadelphia, whilst I was at school, heard me mention Colonel Walton—a most distinguished, religious old la-dy—and said to me, "Henry, my son, you should be ashamed to speak of that old villain or confess that you ever knew him," proceeding to give me his awful, blood-curdling history.

It was mainly a figment of her fancy and prejudice, and I repeated it to Colonel Walton the next time I went to the hotel where he was then living—I have since learned, with a lady not his wife, though he was then three score and ten—and he cried, "That old hag! Good Lord! Don't they ever die!"

Seeing every day the most distinguished public men of the coun-try, and with many of them brought into direct acquaintance by the easy intercourse of hotel life, destroyed any reverence I might have acquired for official station. Familiarity may not always breed con-tempt, but it is a veritable eye opener. To me no divinity hedged the brow of a senator. I knew the White House too well to be impressed by its architectural grandeur without and rather bizarre furnishments within.

VII

I have declaimed not a little in my time about the ignoble trade of politics, the collective dishonesty of parties and the vulgarities of the self-exploiting professional office hunters. Parties are parties. Professional politics and politicians are probably neither worse nor better — barring their pretensions — than other lines of human endeavor. The play actor must be agreeable on the stage of the playhouse; the politician on the highways and the hustings, which constitute his playhouse — all the world a stage — neither to be seriously blamed for the dissimulation which, being an asset, becomes, as it were, a second nature.

The men who between 1850 and 1861 might have saved the Union and averted the War of Sections were on either side professional politicians, with here and there an unselfish, far-seeing, patriotic man, whose admonitions were not heeded by the people ranging on opposing sides of party lines. The two most potential of the party leaders were Mr. Davis and Mr. Seward. The South might have seen and known that the one hope of the institution of slavery lay in the Union. However it ended, disunion led to abolition. The world — the whole trend of modern thought — was set against slavery. But politics, based on party feeling, is a game of blindman's buff. And then — here I show myself a son of Scotland — there is a destiny. "What is to be," says the predestinarian Mother Goose, "will be, though it never come to pass."

That was surely the logic of the irrepressible conflict — only it did come to pass — and for four years millions of people, the most homogeneous, practical and intelligent, fought to a finish a fight over a quiddity; both devoted to liberty, order and law, neither seeking any real change in the character of its organic contract.

Human nature remains ever the same. These days are very like those days. We have had fifty years of a restored Union. The sectional fires have quite gone out. Yet behold the schemes of revolution claiming the regenerative. Most of them call themselves the "uplift!"

Let us agree at once that all government is more or less a failure; society as fraudulent as the satirists describe it; yet, when we turn to the uplift—particularly the professional uplift—what do we find but the same old tunes, hypocrisy and empiricism posing as "friends of the people," preaching the pussy gospel of "sweetness and light?"

"Words, words, words," says Hamlet. Even as veteran writers for the press have come through disheartening experience to a realizing sense of the futility of printer's ink must our academic pundits begin to suspect the futility of art and letters. Words however cleverly writ on paper are after all but words. "In a nation of blind men," we are told, "the one-eyed man is king." In a nation of undiscriminating voters the noise of the agitator is apt to drown the voice of the statesman. We have been teaching everybody to read, nobody to think; and as a consequence—the rule of numbers the law of the land, partyism in the saddle—legislation, state and Federal, becomes largely a matter of riding to hounds and horns. All this, which was true in the fifties, is true to-day.

Under the pretense of "liberalizing" the Government the politicians are sacrificing its organic character to whimsical experimentation; its checks and balances wisely designed to promote and protect liberty are being loosened by schemes of reform more or less visionary; while nowhere do we find intelligence enlightened by experience, and conviction supported by self-control, interposing to save the representative system of the Constitution from the onward march of the proletariat.

One cynic tells us that "A statesman is a politician who is dead," and another cynic varies the epigram to read "A politician out of a job." Patriotism cries "God give us men," but the parties say "Give us votes and offices," and Congress proceeds to create a commission. Thus responsibilities are shirked and places are multiplied.

Assuming, since many do, that the life of nations is mortal even as is the life of man—in all things of growth and decline assimilating—has not our world reached the top of the acclivity, and pausing for a moment may it not be about to take the downward course into another abyss of collapse and oblivion?

The miracles of electricity the last word of science, what is left for man to do? With wireless telegraphy, the airplane and the automobile annihilating time and space, what else? Turning from the material to the ethical it seems of the very nature of the human species to meddle and muddle. On every hand we see the organization of societies for making men and women over again according to certain fantastic images existing in the minds of the promoters. "*Mon Dieu!*" exclaimed the visiting Frenchman. "Fifty religions and only one soup!" Since then both the soups and the religions have multiplied until there is scarce a culinary or moral conception which has not some sect or club to represent it. The uplift is the keynote of these.

Chapter the Third

The Inauguration of Lincoln — I Quit Washington and Return to
Tennessee — A Run-a-bout with Forest — Through the Federal
Lines and a
Dangerous Adventure — Good Luck at Memphis

I

It may have been Louis the Fifteenth, or it may have been Madame de Pompadour, who said, "After me the deluge;" but whichever it was, very much that thought was in Mr. Buchanan's mind in 1861 as the time for his exit from the White House approached. At the North there had been a political ground-swell; at the South, secession, half accomplished by the Gulf States, yawned in the Border States. Curiously enough, very few believed that war was imminent.

As a reporter for the States I met Mr. Lincoln immediately on his arrival in Washington. He came in unexpectedly ahead of the hour announced, to escape, as was given out, a well-laid plan to assassinate him as he passed through Baltimore. I did not believe at the time, and I do not believe now, that there was any real ground for this apprehension.

All through that winter there had been a deal of wild talk. One story had it that Mr. Buchanan was to be kidnapped and made off with so that Vice President Breckenridge might succeed and, acting as *de facto* President, throw the country into confusion and revolution, defeating the inauguration of Lincoln and the coming in of the Republicans. It was a figment of drink and fancy. There was never any such scheme. If there had been Breckenridge would not have consented to be party to it. He was a man of unusual mental as well as personal dignity and both temperamentally and intellectually a thorough conservative.

I had been engaged by Mr. L.A. Gobright, the agent of what became later the Associated Press, to help with the report of the inauguration ceremonies the 4th of March, 1861, and in the discharge of this duty I kept as close to Mr. Lincoln as I could get, following after him from the senate chamber to the east portico of the capitol and standing by his side whilst he delivered his inaugural address.

Perhaps I shall not be deemed prolix if I dwell with some particularity upon an occasion so historic. I had first encountered the newly elected President the afternoon of the day in the early morning of which he had arrived in Washington. It was a Saturday, I think. He came to the capitol under the escort of Mr. Seward, and among the rest I was presented to him. His appearance did not impress me as fantastically as it had impressed some others. I was familiar with the Western type, and whilst Mr. Lincoln was not an Adonis, even after prairie ideals, there was about him a dignity that commanded respect.

I met him again the next Monday forenoon in his apartment at Willard's Hotel as he was preparing to start to his inauguration, and was struck by his unaffected kindness, for I came with a matter requiring his attention. This was, in point of fact, to get from him a copy of the inauguration speech for the Associated Press. I turned it over to Ben Perley Poore, who, like myself, was assisting Mr. Gobright. The President that was about to be seemed entirely self-possessed; not a sign of nervousness, and very obliging. As I have said, I accompanied the cortège that passed from the senate chamber to the east portico. When Mr. Lincoln removed his hat to face the vast throng in front and below, I extended my hand to take it, but Judge Douglas, just behind me, reached over my outstretched arm and received it, holding it during the delivery of the address. I stood just near enough the speaker's elbow not to obstruct any gestures he might make, though he made but few; and then I began to get a suspicion of the power of the man.

He delivered that inaugural address as if he had been delivering inaugural addresses all his life. Firm, resonant, earnest, it an-

nounced the coming of a man, of a leader of men; and in its tone
and style the gentlemen whom he had invited to become members
of his political family—each of whom thought himself a bigger man
than his chief—might have heard the voice and seen the hand of
one born to rule. Whether they did or not, they very soon ascertained the fact. From the hour Abraham Lincoln crossed the threshold of the White House to the hour he went thence to his death,
there was not a moment when he did not dominate the political and
military situation and his official subordinates. The idea that he was
overtopped at any time by anybody is contradicted by all that actually happened.

I was a young Democrat and of course not in sympathy with Mr.
Lincoln or his opinions. Judge Douglas, however, had taken the
edge off my hostility. He had said to me upon his return in triumph
to Washington after the famous Illinois campaign of 1868: "Lincoln
is a good man; in fact, a great man, and by far the ablest debater I
have ever met," and now the newcomer began to verify this opinion
both in his private conversation and in his public attitude.

II

I had been an undoubting Union boy. Neither then nor afterward
could I be fairly classified as a Secessionist. Circumstance rather
than conviction or predilection threw me into the Confederate service, and, being in, I went through with it.

The secession leaders I held in distrust; especially Yancey, Mason,
Slidell, Benjamin and Iverson, Jefferson Davis and Isham G. Harris
were not favorites of mine. Later along I came into familiar association with most of them, and relations were established which may
be described as confidential and affectionate. Lamar and I were
brought together oddly enough in 1869 by Carl Schurz, and thence-
forward we were the most devoted friends. Harris and I fell together in 1862 in the field, first with Forrest and later with Johnston and
Hood, and we remained as brothers to the end, when he closed a

great career in the upper house of Congress, and by Republican votes, though he was a Democrat, as president of the Senate.

He continued in the Governorship of Tennessee through the war. He at no time lost touch with the Tennessee troops, and though not always in the field, never missed a forward movement. In the early spring of 1864, just before the famous Johnston-Sherman campaign opened, General Johnston asked him to go around among the boys and "stir 'em up a bit." The Governor invited me to ride with him. Together we visited every sector in the army. Threading the woods of North Georgia on this round, if I heard it once I heard it fifty times shouted from a distant clearing: "Here comes Gov-ner Harris, fellows; g'wine to be a fight." His appearance at the front had always preceded and been long ago taken as a signal for battle.

[Illustration: John Bell of Tennessee—In 1860 Presidential Candidate "Union Party"—"Bell and Everett" Ticket.]

My being a Washington correspondent of the Philadelphia Press and having lived since childhood at Willard's Hotel, where the Camerons also lived, will furnish the key to my becoming an actual and active rebel. A few days after the inauguration of Mr. Lincoln, Colonel Forney came to my quarters and, having passed the time of day, said: "The Secretary of War wishes you to be at the department to-morrow morning as near nine o'clock as you can make it."

"What does he want, Colonel Forney?" I asked.

"He is going to offer you the position of private secretary to the Secretary of War, with the rank of lieutenant colonel, and I am very desirous that you accept it."

He went away leaving me rather upset. I did not sleep very soundly that night. "So," I argued to myself, "it has come to this, that Forney and Cameron, lifelong enemies, have made friends and are going to rob the Government—one clerk of the House, the other Secretary of War—and I, a mutual choice, am to be the confidential middle man." I still had a home in Tennessee and I rose from my bed, resolved to go there.

I did not keep the proposed appointment for next day. As soon as I could make arrangements I quitted Washington and went to Tennessee, still unchanged in my preconceptions. I may add, since they were verified by events, that I have not modified them from that day to this.

I could not wholly believe with either extreme. I had perpetrated no wrong, but in my small way had done my best for the Union and against secession. I would go back to my books and my literary ambitions and let the storm blow over. It could not last very long; the odds against the South were too great. Vain hope! As well expect a chip on the surface of the ocean to lie quiet as a lad of twenty-one in those days to keep out of one or the other camp. On reaching home I found myself alone. The boys were all gone to the front. The girls were—well, they were all crazy. My native country was about to be invaded. Propinquity. Sympathy. So, casting opinions to the winds in I went on feeling. And that is how I became a rebel, a case of "first endure and then embrace," because I soon got to be a pretty good rebel and went the limit, changing my coat as it were, though not my better judgment, for with a gray jacket on my back and ready to do or die, I retained my belief that secession was treason, that disunion was the height of folly and that the South was bound to go down in the unequal strife.

I think now, as an academic proposition, that, in the doctrine of secession, the secession leaders had a debatable, if not a logical case; but I also think that if the Gulf States had been allowed to go out by tacit consent they would very soon have been back again seeking readmission to the Union.

Man proposes and God disposes. The ways of Deity to man are indeed past finding out. Why, the long and dreadful struggle of a kindred people, the awful bloodshed and havoc of four weary years, leaving us at the close measurably where we were at the beginning, is one of the mysteries which should prove to us that there is a world hereafter, since no great creative principle could produce one with so dire, with so short a span and nothing beyond.

III

The change of parties wrought by the presidential election of 1860 and completed by the coming in of the Republicans in 1861 was indeed revolutionary. When Mr. Lincoln had finished his inaugural address and the crowd on the east portico began to disperse, I reentered the rotunda between Mr. Reverdy Johnson, of Maryland, and Mr. John Bell, of Tennessee, two old friends of my family, and for a little we sat upon a bench, they discussing the speech we had just heard.

Both were sure there would be no war. All would be well, they thought, each speaking kindly of Mr. Lincoln. They were among the most eminent men of the time, I a boy of twenty-one; but to me war seemed a certainty. Recalling the episode, I have often realized how the intuitions of youth outwit the wisdom and baffle the experience of age.

I at once resigned my snug sinecure in the Interior Department and, closing my accounts of every sort, was presently ready to turn my back upon Washington and seek adventures elsewhere.

They met me halfway and came in plenty. I tried staff duty with General Polk, who was making an expedition into Western Kentucky. In a few weeks illness drove me into Nashville, where I passed the next winter in desultory newspaper work. Then Nashville fell, and, as I was making my way out of town afoot and trudging the Murfreesboro pike, Forrest, with his squadron just escaped from Fort Donelson, came thundering by, and I leaped into an empty saddle. A few days later Forrest, promoted to brigadier general, attached me to his staff, and the next six months it was mainly guerilla service, very much to my liking. But Fate, if not Nature, had decided that I was a better writer than fighter, and the Bank of Tennessee having bought a newspaper outfit at Chattanooga, I was sent there to edit The Rebel—my own naming—established as the organ of the Tennessee state government. I made it the organ of the army.

It is not the purpose of these pages to retell the well-known story of the war. My life became a series of ups and downs—mainly downs—the word being from day to day to fire and fall back; in the

Johnston-Sherman campaign, I served as chief of scouts; then as an aid to General Hood through the siege of Atlanta, sharing the beginning of the chapter of disasters that befell that gallant soldier and his army. I was spared the last and worst of these by a curious piece of special duty, taking me elsewhere, to which I was assigned in the autumn of 1864 by the Confederate government.

This involved a foreign journey. It was no less than to go to England to sell to English buyers some hundred thousand bales of designated cotton to be thus rescued from spoliation, acting under the supervision and indeed the orders of the Confederate fiscal agency at Liverpool.

Of course I was ripe for this; but it proved a bigger job than I had conceived or dreamed. The initial step was to get out of the country. But how? That was the question. To run the blockade had been easy enough a few months earlier. All our ports were now sealed by Federal cruisers and gunboats. There was nothing for it but to slip through the North and to get either a New York or a Canadian boat. This involved chances and disguises.

IV

In West Tennessee, not far from Memphis, lived an aunt of mine. Thither I repaired. My plan was to get on a Mississippi steamer calling at one of the landings for wood. This proved impracticable. I wandered many days and nights, rather ill mounted, in search of some kind — any kind — of exit, when one afternoon, quite worn out, I sat by a log heap in a comfortable farmhouse. It seemed that I was at the end of my tether; I did not know what to do.

Presently there was an arrival — a brisk gentleman right out of Memphis, which I then learned was only ten miles distant — bringing with him a morning paper. In this I saw appended to various army orders the name of "N.B. Dana, General Commanding."

That set me to thinking. Was not Dana the name of a certain captain, a stepson of Congressman Peaslee, of New Hampshire, who had lived with us at Willard's Hotel—and were there not two children, Charley and Mamie, and a dear little mother, and—I had been listening to the talk of the newcomer. He was a licensed cotton buyer with a pass to come and go at will through the lines, and was returning next day.

"I want to get into Memphis—I am a nephew of Mrs. General Dana. Can you take me in?" I said to this person.

After some hesitation he consented to try, it being agreed that my mount and outfit should be his if he got me through; no trade if he failed.

Clearly the way ahead was brightening. I soon ascertained that I was with friends, loyal Confederates. Then I told them who I was, and all became excitement for the next day's adventure.

We drove down to the Federal outpost. Crenshaw—that was the name of the cotton buyer—showed his pass to the officer in command, who then turned to me. "Captain," I said, "I have no pass, but I am a nephew of Mrs. General Dana. Can you not pass me in without a pass?" He was very polite. It was a chain picket, he said; his orders were very strict, and so on.

"Well," I said, "suppose I were a member of your own command and were run in here by guerillas. What do you think would it be your duty to do?"

"In that case," he answered, "I should send you to headquarters with a guard."

"Good!" said I. "Can't you send me to headquarters with a guard?"

He thought a moment. Then he called a cavalryman from the outpost.

"Britton," he said, "show this gentleman in to General Dana's headquarters."

Crenshaw lashed his horse and away we went. "That boy thinks he is a guide, not a guard," said he. "You are all right. We can easily get rid of him."

This proved true. We stopped by a saloon and bought a bottle of whisky. When we reached headquarters the lad said, "Do you gentlemen want me any more?" We did not. Then we gave him the bottle of whisky and he disappeared round the corner. "Now you are safe," said Crenshaw. "Make tracks."

But as I turned away and out of sight I began to consider the situation. Suppose that picket on the outpost reported to the provost marshal general that he had passed a relative of Mrs. Dana? What then? Provost guard. Drumhead court-martial. Shot at daylight. It seemed best to play out the hand as I had dealt it. After all, I could make a case if I faced it out.

The guard at the door refused me access to General Dana. Driven by a nearby hackman to the General's residence, and, boldly asking for Mrs. Dana, I was more successful. I introduced myself as a teacher of music seeking to return to my friends in the North, working in a word about the old Washington days, not forgetting "Charley" and "Mamie." The dear little woman was heartily responsive. Both were there, including a pretty girl from Philadelphia, and she called them down. "Here is your old friend, Henry Waterman," she joyfully exclaimed. Then guests began to arrive. It was a reception evening. My hope fell. Some one would surely recognize me. Presently a gentleman entered, and Mrs. Dana said: "Colonel Meehan, this is my particular friend, Henry Waterman, who has been teaching music out in the country, and wants to go up the river. You will give him a pass, I am sure." It was the provost marshal, who answered, "certainly." Now was my time for disappearing. But Mrs. Dana would not listen to this. General Dana would never forgive her if she let me go. Besides, there was to be a supper and a dance. I sat down again very much disconcerted. The situation was becoming awkward. Then Mrs. Dana spoke. "You say you have been teaching music. What is your instrument?" Saved! "The piano," I answered. The girls escorted me to the rear drawing-room. It was a new Steinway Grand, just set up, and I played for my life. If the black bombazine covering my gray uniform did not break, all would be well. I was having a delightfully good time, the girls on either hand, when Mrs. Dana, still enthusiastic, ran in and said, "General Dana is here. Remembers you perfectly. Come and see him."

He stood by a table, tall, sardonic, and as I approached he put out his hand and said: "You have grown a bit, Henry, my boy, since I saw you last. How did you leave my friend Forrest?"

I was about making some awkward reply, when, the room already filling up, he said:

"We have some friends for supper. I am glad you are here. Mamie, my daughter, take Mr. Watterson to the table!"

Lord! That supper! Canvasback! Terrapin! Champagne! The general had seated me at his right. Somewhere toward the close those expressive gray eyes looked at me keenly, and across his wine glass he said:

"I think I understand this. You want to get up the river. You want to see your mother. Have you money enough to carry you through? If you have not don't hesitate, for whatever you need I will gladly let you have."

I thanked him. I had quite enough. All was well. We had more music and some dancing. At a late hour he called the provost marshal.

"Meehan," said he, "take this dangerous young rebel round to the hotel, register him as Smith, Brown, or something, and send him with a pass up the river by the first steamer." I was in luck, was I not?

But I made no impression on those girls. Many years after, meeting Mamie
Dana, as the wife of an army officer at Fortress Monroe, I related the Memphis incident. She did not in the least recall it.

V

I had one other adventure during the war that may be worth telling. It was in 1862. Forrest took it into his inexperienced fighting head to make a cavalry attack upon a Federal stockade, and, repulsed with considerable loss, the command had to disperse—there were not more than two hundred of us—in order to escape capture by the newly-arrived reinforcements that swarmed about. We were to rendezvous later at a certain point. Having some time to spare, and being near the family homestead at Beech Grove, I put in there.

It was midnight when I reached my destination. I had been erroneously informed that the Union Army was on the retreat—quite gone from the neighborhood; and next day, believing the coast was clear, I donned a summer suit and with a neighbor boy who had been wounded at Shiloh and invalided home, rode over to visit some young ladies. We had scarcely been welcomed and were taking a glass of wine when, looking across the lawn, we saw that the place was being surrounded by a body of blue-coats. The story of their departure had been a mistake. They were not all gone.

There was no chance of escape. We were placed in a hollow square and marched across country into camp. Before we got there I had ascertained that they were Indianians, and I was further led rightly to surmise what we called in 1860 Douglas Democrats.

My companion, a husky fellow, who looked and was every inch a soldier, was first questioned by the colonel in command. His examination was brief. He said he was as good a rebel as lived, that he was only waiting for his wound to heal to get back into the Confederate Army, and that if they wanted to hang him for a spy to go ahead.

I was aghast. It was not he that was in danger of hanging, but myself, a soldier in citizen's apparel within the enemy's lines. The colonel turned to me. With what I took for a sneer he said:

"I suppose you are a good Union man?" This offered me a chance.

"That depends upon what you call a good Union man," I answered. "I used to be a very good Union man—a Douglas Democrat—and I am not conscious of having changed my political opinions."

That softened him and we had an old-fashioned, friendly talk about the situation, in which I kept the Douglas Democratic end of it well to the fore. He, too, had been a Douglas Democrat. I soon saw that it was my companion and not myself whom they were after. Presently Colonel Shook, that being the commandant's name, went into the adjacent stockade and the boys about began to be hearty and sympathetic. I made them a regular Douglas Democratic speech. They brought some "red licker" and I asked for some sugar for a toddy, not failing to cite the familiar Sut Lovingood saying that "there were about seventeen round the door who said they'd take sugar in their'n." The drink warmed me to my work, making me quicker, if not bolder, in invention. Then the colonel not reappearing as soon as I hoped he would, for all along my fear was the wires, I went to him.

"Colonel Shook," I said, "you need not bother about this friend of mine. He has no real idea of returning to the Confederate service. He is teaching school over here at Beech Grove and engaged to be married to one of the — girls. If you carry him off a prisoner he will be exchanged back into the fighting line, and we make nothing by it. There is a hot luncheon waiting for us at the — —'s. Leave him to me and I will be answerable." Then I left him.

Directly he came out and said: "I may be doing wrong, and don't feel entirely sure of my ground, but I am going to let you gentlemen go."

We thanked him and made off amid the cheery good-bys of the assembled blue-coats.

No lunch for us. We got to our horses, rode away, and that night I was at our rendezvous to tell the tale to those of my comrades who had arrived before me.

Colonel Shook and I met after the war at a Grand Army reunion where I was billed to speak and to which he introduced me, relating the incident and saying, among other things: "I do believe that when he told me near Wartrace that day twenty years ago that he was a good Union man he told at least half the truth."

Chapter the Fourth

I Go to London—Am Introduced to a Notable Set—
Huxley, Spencer, Mill and Tyndall—Artemus Ward
Comes to Town—The Savage Club

I

The fall of Atlanta after a siege of nearly two months was, in the opinion of thoughtful people, the sure precursor of the fall of the doomed Confederacy. I had an affectionate regard for General Hood, but it was my belief that neither he nor any other soldier could save the day, and being out of commission and having no mind for what I conceived aimless campaigning through another winter—especially an advance into Tennessee upon Nashville—I wrote to an old friend of mine, who owned the Montgomery Mail, asking for a job. He answered that if I would come right along and take the editorship of the paper he would make me a present of half of it—a proposal so opportune and tempting that forty-eight hours later saw me in the capital of Alabama.

I was accompanied by my fidus Achates, Albert Roberts. The morning after our arrival, by chance I came across a printed line which advertised a room and board for two "single gentlemen," with the curious affix for those times, "references will be given and required." This latter caught me. When I rang the visitors' bell of a pretty dwelling upon one of the nearby streets a distinguished gentleman in uniform came to the door, and, acquainted with my business, he said, "Ah, that is an affair of my wife," and invited me within.

He was obviously English. Presently there appeared a beautiful lady, likewise English and as obviously a gentlewoman, and an hour later my friend Roberts and I moved in. The incident proved in many ways fateful. The military gentleman proved to be Doctor Scott, the post surgeon. He was, when we came to know him, the most interesting of men, a son of that Captain Scott who command-ed Byron's flagship at Missolonghi in 1823; had as a lad attended the poet and he in his last illness and been in at the death, seeing the club foot when the body was prepared for burial. His wife was adorable. There were two girls and two boys. To make a long story short, Albert Roberts married one of the daughters, his brother the other; the lads growing up to be successful and distinguished men—one a naval admiral, the other a railway president. When, just after the war, I was going abroad, Mrs. Scott said: "I have a brother living in London to whom I will be glad to give you a letter."

II

Upon the deck of the steamer bound from New York to London direct, as we, my wife and I newly married, were taking a last look at the receding American shore, there appeared a gentleman who seemed by the cut of his jib startlingly French. We had under our escort a French governess returning to Paris. In a twinkle she and this gentleman had struck up an acquaintance, and much to my displeasure she introduced him to me as "Monsieur Mahoney." I was somewhat mollified when later we were made acquainted with Madame Mahoney.

I was not at all preconceived in his favor, nor did Monsieur Ma-honey, upon nearer approach, conciliate my simple taste. In person, manners and apparel he was quite beyond me. Mrs. Mahoney, however, as we soon called her, was a dear, whole-souled, traveled, unaffected New England woman. But Monsieur! Lord! There was no holding him at arm's length. He brooked not resistance. I was wearing a full beard. He said it would never do, carried me perforce below, and cut it as I have worn it ever since. The day before we were to dock he took me aside and said:

"Mee young friend" — he had a brogue which thirty years in Algiers, where he had been consul, and a dozen in Paris as a gentleman of leisure, had not wholly spoiled — "Mee young friend, I observe that you are shy of strangers, but my wife and I have taken a shine to you and the 'Princess'," as he called Mrs. Watterson, "and if you will allow us, we can be of some sarvis to you when we get to town."

Certainly there was no help for it. I was too ill of the long crossing to oppose him. At Blackwall we took the High Level for Fenchurch Street, at Fenchurch Street a cab for the West End — Mr. Mahoney bossing the job — and finally, in most comfortable and inexpensive lodgings, we were settled in Jermyn Street. The Mahoneys were visiting Lady Elmore, widow of a famous surgeon and mother of the President of the Royal Academy. Thus we were introduced to quite a distinguished artistic set.

It was great. It was glorious. At last we were in London — the dream of my literary ambitions. I have since lived much in this wondrous city and in many parts of it between Hyde Park Corner, the heart of May Fair, to the east end of Bloomsbury under the very sound of Bow Bells. All the way as it were from Tyburn Tree that was, and the Marble Arch that is, to Charing Cross and the Hay Market. This were not to mention casual sojourns along Piccadilly and the Strand.

In childhood I was obsessed by the immensity, the atmosphere and the mystery of London. Its nomenclature embedded itself in my fancy; Hounsditch and Shoreditch, Billingsgate and Blackfriars; Bishopgate, within, and Bishopgate, without; Threadneedle Street and Wapping-Old-Stairs; the Inns of Court where Jarndyce struggled with Jarndyce, and the taverns where the Mark Tapleys, the Captain Costigans and the Dolly Vardens consorted.

Alike in winter fog and summer haze, I grew to know and love it, and those that may be called its dramatis personae, especially its tatterdemalions, the long procession led by Jack Sheppard, Dick Turpin and Jonathan Wild the Great. Inevitably I sought their haunts — and they were not all gone in those days; the Bull-and-Gate in Holborn, whither Mr. Tom Jones repaired on his arrival in town, and the White Hart Tavern, where Mr. Pickwick fell in with Mr.

Sam Weller; the regions about Leicester Fields and Russell Square sacred to the memory of Captain Booth and the lovely Amelia and Becky Sharp; where Garrick drank tea with Dr. Johnson and Henry Esmond tippled with Sir Richard Steele. There was yet a Pump Court, and many places along Oxford Street where Mantalini and De Quincy loitered: and Covent Garden and Drury Lane. Evans' Coffee House, or shall I say the Cave of Harmony, and The Cock and the Cheshire Cheese were near at hand for refreshment in the agreeable society of Daniel Defoe and Joseph Addison, with Oliver Goldsmith and Dick Swiveller and Colonel Newcome to clink ghostly glasses amid the punch fumes and tobacco smoke. In short I knew London when it was still Old London — the knowledge of Temple Bar and Cheapside — before the vandal horde of progress and the pickaxe of the builder had got in their nefarious work.

III

Not long after we began our sojourn in London, I recurred — by chance, I am ashamed to say — to Mrs. Scott's letter of introduction to her brother. The address read "Mr. Thomas H. Huxley, School of Mines, Jermyn Street." Why, it was but two or three blocks away, and being so near I called, not knowing just who Mr. Thomas H. Huxley might be.

I was conducted to a dark, stuffy little room. The gentleman who met me was exceedingly handsome and very agreeable. He greeted me cordially and we had some talk about his relatives in America. Of course my wife and I were invited at once to dinner. I was a little perplexed. There was no one to tell me about Huxley, or in what way he might be connected with the School of Mines.

It was a good dinner. There sat at table a gentleman by the name of Tyndall and another by the name of Mill — of neither I had ever heard — but there was still another of the name of Spencer, whom I fancied must be a literary man, for I recalled having reviewed a clever book on Education some four years agone by a writer of that name; a certain Herbert Spencer, whom I rightly judged might he be.

The dinner, I repeat, was a very good dinner indeed—the Huxleys, I took it, must be well to do—the company agreeable; a bit pragmatic, however, I thought. The gentleman by the name of Spencer said he loved music and wished to hear Mrs. Watterson sing, especially Longfellow's Rainy Day, and left the others of us—Huxley, Mill, Tyndall and myself—at table. Finding them a little off on the Irish question as well as American affairs, I set them right as to both with much particularity and a great deal of satisfaction to myself.

Whatever Huxley's occupation, it turned out that he had at least one book-publishing acquaintance, Mr. Alexander Macmillan, to whom he introduced me next day, for I had brought with me a novel—the great American romance—too good to be wasted on New York, Philadelphia or Boston, but to appear simultaneously in England and the United States, to be translated, of course, into French, Italian and German. This was actually accepted. It was held for final revision.

We were to pass the winter in Italy. An event, however, called me suddenly home. Politics and journalism knocked literature sky high, and the novel—it was entitled "One Story's Good Till Another Is Told"—was laid by and quite forgotten. Some twenty years later, at a moment when I was being lashed from one end of the line to the other, my wife said:

"Let us drop the nasty politics and get back to literature." She had preserved the old manuscript, two thousand pages of it.

"Fetch it," I said.

She brought it with effulgent pride. Heavens! The stuff it was! Not a gleam, never a radiance. I had been teaching myself to write—I had been writing for the English market—perpendicular! The Lord has surely been good to me. If the "boys" had ever got a peep at that novel, I had been lost indeed!

IV

Yea, verily we were in London. Presently Artemus Ward and "the show" arrived in town. He took a lodging over an apothecary's just across the way from Egyptian Hall in Piccadilly, where he was to lecture. We had been the best of friends, were near of an age, and only round-the-corner apart we became from the first inseparable. I introduced him to the distinguished scientific set into which chance had thrown me, and he introduced me to a very different set that made a revel of life at the Savage Club.

I find by reference to some notes jotted down at the time that the last I saw of him was the evening of the 21st of December, 1866. He had dined with my wife and myself, and, accompanied by Arthur Sketchley, who had dropped in after dinner, he bade us good-by and went for his nightly grind, as he called it. We were booked to take our departure the next morning. His condition was pitiable. He was too feeble to walk alone, and was continually struggling to breathe freely. His surgeon had forbidden the use of wine or liquor of any sort. Instead he drank quantities of water, eating little and taking no exercise at all. Nevertheless, he stuck to his lecture and contrived to keep up appearances before the crowds that flocked to hear him, and even in London his critical state of health was not suspected.

Early in September, when I had parted from him to go to Paris, I left him methodically and industriously arranging for his début. He had brought some letters, mainly to newspaper people, and was already making progress toward what might be called the interior circles of the press, which are so essential to the success of a new-comer in London. Charles Reade and Andrew Haliday became zealous friends. It was to the latter that he owed his introduction to the Savage Club. Here he soon made himself at home. His manners, even his voice, were half English, albeit he possessed a most engaging disposition—a ready tact and keen discernment, very un-English,—and these won him an efficient corps of claquers and backers throughout the newspapers and periodicals of the metropolis. Thus his success was assured from the first.

The raw November evening when he opened at Egyptian Hall the room was crowded with an audience of literary men and women, great and small, from Swinburne and Edmund Yates to the trumpeters and reporters of the morning papers. The next day most of these contained glowing accounts. The Times was silent, but four days later The Thunderer, seeing how the wind blew, came out with a column of eulogy, and from this onward, each evening proved a kind of ovation. Seats were engaged for a week in advance. Up and down Piccadilly, from St. James Church to St. James Street, carriages bearing the first arms in the kingdom were parked night after night; and the evening of the 21st of December, six weeks after, there was no falling off. The success was complete. As to an American, London had never seen the like.

All this while the poor author of the sport was slowly dying. The demands upon his animal spirits at the Savage Club, the bodily fatigue of "getting himself up to it," the "damnable iteration" of the lecture itself, wore him out. George, his valet, whom he had brought from America, had finally to lift him about his bedroom like a child. His quarters in Picadilly, as I have said, were just opposite the Hall, but he could not go backward and forward without assistance. It was painful in the extreme to see the man who was undergoing tortures behind the curtain step lightly before the audience amid a burst of merriment, and for more than an hour sustain the part of jester, tossing his cap and jingling his bells, a painted death's head, for he had to rouge his face to hide the pallor.

His buoyancy forsook him. He was occasionally nervous and fretful. The fog, he declared, felt like a winding sheet, enwrapping and strangling him. At one of his entertainments he made a grim, serio-comic allusion to this. "But," cried he as he came off the stage, "that was not a hit, was it? The English are scary about death. I'll have to cut it out."

He had become a contributor to Punch, a lucky rather than smart business stroke, for it was not of his own initiation. He did not continue his contributions after he began to appear before the public, and the discontinuance was made the occasion of some ill-natured remarks in certain American papers, which very much wounded him. They were largely circulated and credited at the time, the charge being that Messrs. Bradbury and Evans, the publishers of the English charivari, had broken with him because the English would not have him. The truth is that their original proposal was made to him, not by him to them, the price named being fifteen guineas a letter. He asked permission to duplicate the arrangement with some New York periodical, so as to secure an American copyright. This they refused. I read the correspondence at the time. "Our aim," they said, "in making the engagement, had reference to our own circulation in the United States, which exceeds twenty-seven thousand weekly."

I suggested to Artemus that he enter his book, "Artemus Ward in London," in advance, and he did write to Oakey Hall, his New York lawyer, to that effect. Before he received an answer from Hall he got Carleton's advertisement announcing the book. Considering this a piratical design on the part of Carleton, he addressed that enterprising publisher a savage letter, but the matter was ultimately cleared up to his satisfaction, for he said just before we parted: "It was all a mistake about Carleton. I did him an injustice and mean to ask his pardon. He has behaved very handsomely to me." Then the letters reappeared in Punch.

V

Whatever may be thought of them on this side of the Atlantic, their success in England was undeniable. They were more talked about than any current literary matter; never a club gathering or dinner party at which they were not discussed. There did seem something both audacious and grotesque in this ruthless Yankee poking in among the revered antiquities of Britain, so that the beef-eating British themselves could not restrain their laughter. They took his jokes in excellent part. The letters on the Tower and Chawsir were palpable hits, and it was generally agreed that Punch had contained nothing better since the days of Yellow-plush. This opinion was not confined to the man in the street. It was shared by the high-brows of the reviews and the appreciative of society, and gained Artemus the entrée wherever he cared to go.

Invitations pursued him and he was even elected to two or three fashionable clubs. But he had a preference for those which were less conventional. His admission to the Garrick, which had been at first "laid over," affords an example of London club fastidiousness. The gentleman who proposed him used his pseudonym, Artemus Ward, instead of his own name, Charles F. Browne. I had the pleasure of introducing him to Mr. Alexander Macmillan, the famous book publisher of Oxford and Cambridge, a leading member of the Garrick. We dined together at the Garrick clubhouse, when the matter was brought up and explained. The result was that Charles F. Browne was elected at the next meeting, where Artemus Ward, had been made to stand aside.

Before Christmas, Artemus received invitations from distinguished people, nobility and gentry as well as men of letters, to spend the week-end with them. But he declined them all. He needed his vacation, he said, for rest. He had neither the strength nor the spirit for the season.

Yet was he delighted with the English people and with English life. His was one of those receptive natures which enjoy whatever is wholesome and sunny. In spite of his bodily pain, he entertained a lively hope of coming out of it in the spring, and did not realize his true condition. He merely said, "I have overworked myself, and must lay by or I shall break down altogether." He meant to remain in London as long as his welcome lasted, and when he perceived a falling off in his audience, would close his season and go to the continent. His receipts averaged about three hundred dollars a night, whilst his expenses were not fifty dollars. "This, mind you," he used to say, "is in very hard cash, an article altogether superior to that of my friend Charles Reade."

[Illustration: Artemas Ward]

His idea was to set aside out of his earnings enough to make him independent, and then to give up "this mountebank business," as he called it. He had a great respect for scholarly culture and personal respectability, and thought that if he could get time and health he might do something "in the genteel comedy line." He had a humorous novel in view, and a series of more aspiring comic essays than any he had attempted.

Often he alluded to the opening for an American magazine, "not quite so highfalutin as the Atlantic nor so popular as Harper's." His mind was beginning to soar above the showman and merrymaker. His manners had always been captivating. Except for the nervous worry of ill-health, he was the kind-hearted, unaffected Artemus of old, loving as a girl and liberal as a prince. He once showed me his daybook in which were noted down over five hundred dollars lent out in small sums to indigent Americans.

"Why," said I, "you will never get half of it back."

"Of course not," he said, "but do you think I can afford to have a lot of loose fellows black-guarding me at home because I wouldn't let them have a sovereign or so over here?"

There was no lack of independence, however, about him. The benefit which he gave Mrs. Jefferson Davis in New Orleans, which was denounced at the North as toadying to the Rebels, proceeded from a wholly different motive. He took a kindly interest in the case because it was represented to him as one of suffering, and knew very well at the time that his bounty would meet with detraction.

He used to relate with gusto an interview he once had with Murat Halstead, who had printed a tart paragraph about him. He went into the office of the Cincinnati editor, and began in his usual jocose way to ask for the needful correction. Halstead resented the proffered familiarity, when Artemus told him flatly, suddenly changing front, that he "didn't care a d—n for the Commercial, and the whole establishment might go to hell." Next day the paper appeared with a handsome amende, and the two became excellent friends. "I have no doubt," said Artemus, "that if I had whined or begged, I should have disgusted Halstead, and he would have put it to me tighter. As it was, he concluded that I was not a sneak, and treated me like a gentleman."

Artemus received many tempting offers from book publishers in London. Several of the Annuals for 1866-67 contain sketches, some of them anonymous, written by him, for all of which he was well paid. He wrote for Fun—the editor of which, Mr. Tom Hood, son of the great humorist, was an intimate friend — as well as for Punch; his contributions to the former being printed without his signature. If he had been permitted to remain until the close of his season, he would have earned enough, with what he had already, to attain the independence which was his aim and hope. His best friends in London were Charles Reade, Tom Hood, Tom Robertson, the dramatist, Charles Mathews, the comedian, Tom Taylor and Arthur Sketchley. He did not meet Mr. Dickens, though Mr. Andrew Haliday, Dickens' familiar, was also his intimate. He was much persecuted by lion hunters, and therefore had to keep his lodgings something of a mystery.

So little is known of Artemus Ward that some biographic particulars may not in this connection be out of place or lacking in interest.

Charles F. Browne was born at Waterford, Maine, the 15th of July, 1833. His father was a state senator, a probate judge, and at one time a wealthy citizen; but at his death, when his famous son was yet a lad, left his family little or no property. Charles apprenticed himself to a printer, and served out his time, first in Springfield and then in Boston. In the latter city he made the acquaintance of Shilaber, Ben Perley Poore, Halpine, and others, and tried his hand as a "sketchist" for a volume edited by Mrs. Partington. His early effusions bore the signature of "Chub." From the Hub he emigrated to the West. At Toledo, Ohio, he worked as a "typo" and later as a "local" on a Toledo newspaper. Then he went to Cleveland, where as city editor of the Plain Dealer he began the peculiar vein from which still later he worked so successfully.

The soubriquet "Artemus Ward," was not taken from the Revolutionary general. It was suggested by an actual personality. In an adjoining town to Cleveland there was a snake charmer who called himself Artemus Ward, an ignorant witling or half-wit, the laughing stock of the countryside. Browne's first communication over the signature of Artemus Ward purported to emanate from this person, and it succeeded so well that he kept it up. He widened the conception as he progressed. It was not long before his sketches began to be copied and he became a newspaper favorite. He remained in Cleveland from 1857 to 1860, when he was called to New York to take the editorship of a venture called Vanity Fair. This died soon after. But he did not die with it. A year later, in the fall of 1861, he made his appearance as a lecturer at New London, and met with encouragement. Then he set out *en tour*, returned to the metropolis, hired a hall and opened with "the show." Thence onward all went well.

The first money he made was applied to the purchase of the old family homestead in Maine, which he presented to his mother. The payments on this being completed, he bought himself a little nest on the Hudson, meaning, as he said, to settle down and perhaps to marry. But his dreams were not destined to be fulfilled.

Thus, at the outset of a career from which much was to be expected, a man, possessed of rare and original qualities of head and heart, sank out of the sphere in which at that time he was the most prominent figure. There was then no Mark Twain or Bret Harte. His rivals were such humorists as Orpheus C. Kerr, Nasby, Asa Hartz, The Fat Contributor, John Happy, Mrs. Partington, Bill Arp and the like, who are now mostly forgotten.

Artemus Ward wrote little, but he made good and left his mark. Along with the queer John Phoenix his writings survived the deluge that followed them. He poured out the wine of life in a limpid stream. It may be fairly said that he did much to give permanency and respectability to the style of literature of which he was at once a brilliant illustrator and illustration. His was a short life indeed, though a merry one, and a sad death. In a strange land, yet surrounded by admiring friends, about to reach the coveted independence he had looked forward to so long, he sank to rest, his dust mingling with that of the great Thomas Hood, alongside of whom he was laid in Kensal Green.

Chapter the Fifth

Mark Twain — The Original of Colonel Mulberry Sellers — The "Earl of
Durham" — Some Noctes Ambrosianæ — A Joke on Murat Halstead

I

Mark Twain came down to the footlights long after Artemus Ward had passed from the scene; but as an American humorist with whom during half a century I was closely intimate and round whom many of my London experiences revolve, it may be apropos to speak of him next after his elder. There was not lacking a certain likeness between them.

Samuel L. Clemens and I were connected by a domestic tie, though before either of us were born the two families on the maternal side had been neighbors and friends. An uncle of his married an aunt of mine — the children of this marriage cousins in common to us — albeit, this apart, we were life-time cronies. He always contended that we were "bloodkin."

Notwithstanding that when Mark Twain appeared east of the Alleghanies and north of the Blue Ridge he showed the weather-beating of the west, the bizarre alike of the pilot house and the mining camp very much in evidence, he came of decent people on both sides of the house. The Clemens and the Lamptons were of good old English stock. Toward the middle of the eighteenth century three younger scions of the Manor of Durham migrated from the County of Durham to Virginia and thence branched out into Tennessee, Kentucky and Missouri.

His mother was the loveliest old aristocrat with a taking drawl, a drawl that was high-bred and patrician, not rustic and plebeian, which her famous son inherited. All the women of that ilk were gentlewomen. The literary and artistic instinct which attained its fruition in him had percolated through the veins of a long line of silent singers, of poets and painters, unborn to the world of expression till he arrived upon the scene.

These joint cousins of ours embraced an exceedingly large, varied and picturesque assortment. Their idiosyncrasies were a constant source of amusement to us. Just after the successful production of his play, The Gilded Age, and the uproarious hit of the comedian, Raymond, in the leading role, I received a letter from him in which he told me he had made in Colonel Mulberry Sellers a close study of one of these kinsmen and thought he had drawn him to the life. "But for the love o' God," he said, "don't whisper it, for he would never understand or forgive me, if he did not thrash me on sight."

The pathos of the part, and not its comic aspects, had most impressed him. He designed and wrote it for Edwin Booth. From the first and always he was disgusted by the Raymond portrayal. Except for its popularity and money-making, he would have withdrawn it from the stage as, in a fit of pique, Raymond himself did while it was still packing the theaters.

The original Sellers had partly brought him up and had been very good to him. A second Don Quixote in appearance and not unlike the knight of La Mancha in character, it would have been safe for nobody to laugh at James Lampton, or by the slightest intimation, look or gesture to treat him with inconsideration, or any proposal of his, however preposterous, with levity.

He once came to visit me upon a public occasion and during a function. I knew that I must introduce him, and with all possible ceremony, to my colleagues. He was very queer; tall and peaked, wearing a black, swallow-tailed suit, shiny with age, and a silk hat, bound with black crepe to conceal its rustiness, not to indicate a recent death; but his linen as spotless as new-fallen snow. I had my fears. Happily the company, quite dazed by the apparition, proved decorous to solemnity, and the kind old gentleman, pleased with himself and proud of his "distinguished young kinsman," went away highly gratified.

Not long after this one of his daughters—pretty girls they were, too, and in charm altogether worthy of their Cousin Sam Clemens—was to be married, and Sellers wrote me a stately summons, all-embracing, though stiff and formal, such as a baron of the Middle Ages might have indited to his noble relative, the field marshal, bidding him bring his good lady and his retinue and abide within the castle until the festivities were ended, though in this instance the castle was a suburban cottage scarcely big enough to accommodate the bridal couple. I showed the bombastic but hospitable and genuine invitation to the actor Raymond, who chanced to be playing in Louisville when it reached me. He read it through with care and reread it.

"Do you know," said he, "it makes me want to cry. That is not the man I am trying to impersonate at all."

Be sure it was not; for there was nothing funny about the spiritual being of Mark Twain's Colonel Mulberry Sellers; he was as brave as a lion and as upright as Sam Clemens himself.

When a very young man, living in a woodland cabin down in the Pennyrile region of Kentucky, with a wife he adored and two or three small children, he was so carried away by an unexpected windfall that he lingered overlong in the nearby village, dispensing a royal hospitality; in point of fact, he "got on a spree." Two or three days passed before he regained possession of himself. When at last he reached home, he found his wife ill in bed and the children nearly starved for lack of food. He said never a word, but walked out of the cabin, tied himself to a tree, and was wildly horsewhipping himself when the cries of the frightened family summoned the neighbors and he was brought to reason. He never touched an intoxicating drop from that day to his death.

Another one of our fantastic mutual cousins was the "Earl of Durham." I ought to say that Mark Twain and I grew up on old wives' tales of estates and titles, which, maybe due to a kindred sense of humor in both of us, we treated with shocking irreverence. It happened some fifty years ago that there turned up, first upon the plains and afterward in New York and Washington, a lineal descendant of the oldest of the Virginia Lamptons—he had somehow gotten hold of or had fabricated a bundle of documents—who was what a certain famous American would have called a "corker." He wore a sombrero with a rattlesnake for a band, and a belt with a couple of six-shooters, and described himself and claimed to be the Earl of Durham.

"He touched me for a tenner the first time I ever saw him," drawled Mark to me, "and I coughed it up and have been coughing them up, whenever he's around, with punctuality and regularity."

The "Earl" was indeed a terror, especially when he had been drinking. His belief in his peerage was as absolute as Colonel Sellers' in his millions. All he wanted was money enough "to get over there" and "state his case." During the Tichborne trial Mark Twain and I were in London, and one day he said to me:

"I have investigated this Durham business down at the Herald's office. There's nothing to it. The Lamptons passed out of the Demesne of Durham a hundred years ago. They had long before dissipated the estates. Whatever the title, it lapsed. The present earldom is a new creation, not the same family at all. But, I tell you what, if you'll put up five hundred dollars I'll put up five hundred more, we'll fetch our chap across and set him in as a claimant, and, my word for it, Kenealy's fat boy won't be a marker to him!"

He was so pleased with his conceit that later along he wrote a novel and called it The Claimant. It is the only one of his books, though I never told him so, that I could not enjoy. Many years after, I happened to see upon a hotel register in Rome these entries: "The Earl of Durham," and in the same handwriting just below it, "Lady Anne Lambton" and "The Hon. Reginald Lambton." So the Lambtons — they spelled it with a b instead of a p — were yet in the peerage. A Lambton was Earl of Durham. The next time I saw Mark I rated him on his deception. He did not defend himself, said something about its being necessary to perfect the joke.

"Did you ever meet this present peer and possible usurper?" I asked.

"No," he answered, "I never did, but if he had called on me, I would have had him come up."

III

His mind turned ever to the droll. Once in London I was living with my family at 103 Mount Street. Between 103 and 102 there was the parochial workhouse, quite a long and imposing edifice. One evening, upon coming in from an outing, I found a letter he had written on the sitting-room table. He had left it with his card. He spoke of the shock he had received upon finding that next to 102 — presumably 103 — was the workhouse. He had loved me, but had always feared that I would end by disgracing the family — being hanged or something — but the "work'us," that was beyond him; he had not thought it would come to that. And so on through pages of horseplay; his relief on ascertaining the truth and learning his mistake, his regret at not finding me at home, closing with a dinner invitation.

It was at Geneva, Switzerland, that I received a long, overflowing letter, full of flamboyant oddities, written from London. Two or three hours later came a telegram. "Burn letter. Blot it from your memory. Susie is dead."

How much of melancholy lay hidden behind the mask of his humour it would be hard to say. His griefs were tempered by a vein of stoicism. He was a medley of contradictions. Unconventional to the point of eccentricity, his sense of his proper dignity was sound and sufficient. Though lavish in the use of money, he had a full realization of its value and made close contracts for his work. Like Sellers, his mind soared when it sailed financial currents. He lacked acute business judgment in the larger things, while an excellent economist in the lesser.

His marriage was the most brilliant stroke of his life. He got the woman of all the world he most needed, a truly lovely and wise helpmate, who kept him in bounds and headed him straight and right while she lived. She was the best of housewives and mothers, and the safest of counsellors and critics. She knew his worth; she appreciated his genius; she understood his limitations and angles. Her death was a grievous disaster as well as a staggering blow. He never wholly recovered from it.

IV

It was in the early seventies that Mark Twain dropped into New York, where there was already gathered a congenial group to meet and greet him. John Hay, quoting old Jack Dade's description of himself, was wont to speak of this group as "of high aspirations and peregrinations." It radiated between Franklin Square, where Joseph W. Harper—"Joe Brooklyn," we called him—reigned in place of his uncle, Fletcher Harper, the man of genius among the original Harper Brothers, and the Lotos Club, then in Irving Place, and Delmonico's, at the corner of Fifth Avenue and Fourteenth Street, with Sutherland's in Liberty Street for a downtown place of luncheon resort, not to forget Dorlon's in Fulton Market.

[Illustration: General Leonidas Polk—Lieutenant General C.S.A.—Killed in
Georgia June 14, 1864—P.E. Bishop of Louisiana]

The Harper contingent, beside its chief, embraced Tom Nast and William A. Seaver, whom John Russell Young named "Papa Pendennis," and pictured as "a man of letters among men of the world and a man of the world among men of letters," a very apt phrase appropriated from Doctor Johnson, and Major Constable, a giant, who looked like a dragoon and not a bookman, yet had known Sir Walter Scott and was sprung from the family of Edinburgh publishers. Bret Harte had but newly arrived from California. Whitelaw Reid, though still subordinate to Greeley, was beginning to make himself felt in journalism. John Hay played high priest to the revels. Occasionally I made a pious pilgrimage to the delightful shrine.

Truth to tell, it emulated rather the gods than the graces, though all of us had literary leanings of one sort and another, especially late at night; and Sam Bowles would come over from Springfield and Murat Halstead from Cincinnati to join us. Howells, always something of a prig, living in Boston, held himself at too high account; but often we had Joseph Jefferson, then in the heyday of his career, with once in a while Edwin Booth, who could not quite trust himself to go our gait. The fine fellows we caught from oversea were innumerable, from the elder Sothern and Sala and Yates to Lord Dufferin and Lord Houghton. Times went very well those days, and whilst some looked on askance, notably Curtis and, rather oddly, Stedman, and thought we were wasting time and convivializing more than was good for us, we were mostly young and hearty, ranging from thirty to five and forty years of age, with amazing capabilities both for work and play, and I cannot recall that any hurt to any of us came of it.

Although robustious, our fribbles were harmless enough — ebullitions of animal spirit, sometimes perhaps of gaiety unguarded — though each shade, treading the Celestian way, as most of them do, and recurring to those Noctes Ambrosianæ, might e'en repeat to the other the words on a memorable occasion addressed by Curran to Lord Avonmore:

"We spent them not in toys or lust or wine;
But search of deep philosophy,
Wit, eloquence and poesy —
Arts which I loved, for they, my friend, were thine."

V

Mark Twain was the life of every company and all occasions. I remember a practical joke of his suggestion played upon Murat Halstead. A party of us were supping after the theater at the old Brevoort House. A card was brought to me from a reporter of the World. I was about to deny myself, when Mark Twain said:

"Give it to me, I'll fix it," and left the table.

Presently he came to the door and beckoned me out.

"I represented myself as your secretary and told this man," said he, "that you were not here, but that if Mr. Halstead would answer just as well I would fetch him. The fellow is as innocent as a lamb and doesn't know either of you. I am going to introduce you as Halstead and we'll have some fun."

No sooner said than done. The reporter proved to be a little bald-headed cherub newly arrived from the isle of dreams, and I lined out to him a column or more of very hot stuff, reversing Halstead in every opinion. I declared him in favor of paying the national debt in greenbacks. Touching the sectional question, which was then the burning issue of the time, I made the mock Halstead say: "The 'bloody shirt' is only a kind of Pickwickian battle cry. It is convenient during political campaigns and on election day. Perhaps you do not know that I am myself of dyed-in-the-wool Southern and secession stock. My father and grandfather came to Ohio from South Carolina just before I was born. Naturally I have no sectional prejudices, but I live in Cincinnati and I am a Republican."

There was not a little more of the same sort. Just how it passed through the World office I know not; but it actually appeared. On returning to the table I told the company what Mark Twain and I had done. They thought I was joking. Without a word to any of us, next day Halstead wrote a note to the World repudiating the interview, and the World printed his disclaimer with a line which said: "When Mr. Halstead conversed with our reporter he had dined." It was too good to keep. A day or two later, John Hay wrote an amusing story for the Tribune, which set Halstead right.

Mark Twain's place in literature is not for me to fix. Some one has called him "The Lincoln of letters." That is striking, suggestive and apposite. The genius of Clemens and the genius of Lincoln possessed a kinship outside the circumstances of their early lives; the common lack of tools to work with; the privations and hardships to be endured and to overcome; the way ahead through an unblazed and trackless forest; every footstep over a stumbling block and each effort saddled with a handicap. But they got there, both of them, they got there, and mayhap somewhere beyond the stars the light of their eyes is shining down upon us even as, amid the thunders of a world tempest, we are not wholly forgetful of them.

Chapter the Sixth

Houston and Wigfall of Texas — Stephen A. Douglas — The Twaddle about
Puritans and Cavaliers — Andrew Johnson and John C. Breckenridge

I

The National Capitol — old men's fancies fondly turn to thoughts of youth — was picturesque in its personalities if not in its architecture. By no means the least striking of these was General and Senator Sam Houston, of Texas. In his life of adventure truth proved very much stranger than fiction.

The handsomest of men, tall and stately, he could pass no way without attracting attention; strangers in the Senate gallery first asked to have him pointed out to them, and seeing him to all appearance idling his time with his jacknife and bits of soft wood which he whittled into various shapes of hearts and anchors for distribution among his lady acquaintances, they usually went away thinking him a queer old man. So inded he was; yet on his feet and in action singularly impressive, and, when he chose, altogether the statesman and orator.

There united in him the spirits of the troubadour and the spearman. Ivanhoe was not more gallant nor Bois-Guilbert fiercer. But the valor and the prowess were tempered by humor. Below the surging subterranean flood that stirred and lifted him to high attempt, he was a comedian who had tales to tell, and told them wondrous well. On a lazy summer afternoon on the shady side of Willard's Hotel — the Senate not in session — he might be seen, an admiring group about him, spinning these yarns, mostly of personal experience—rarely if ever repeating himself—and in tone, gesture and grimace reproducing the drolleries of the backwoods, which from boyhood had been his home.

He spared not himself. According to his own account he had been in the early days of his Texas career a drunkard. "Everybody got drunk," I once heard him say, referring to the beginning of the Texas revolution, as he gave a side-splitting picture of that bloody episode, "and I realized that somebody must get sober and keep sober."

From the hour of that realization, when he "swore off," to the hour of his death he never touched intoxicants of any sort.

He had fought under Jackson, had served two terms in Congress and had been elected governor of Tennessee before he was forty. Then he fell in love. The young lady was a beautiful girl, well-born and highly educated, a schoolmate of my mother's elder sister. She was persuaded by her family to throw over an obscure young man whom she preferred, and to marry a young man so eligible and distinguished.

He took her to Nashville, the state capital. There were rounds of gayety. Three months passed. Of a sudden the little town woke to the startling rumor, which proved to be true, that the brilliant young couple had come to a parting of the ways. The wife had returned to her people. The husband had resigned his office and was gone, no one knew where.

A few years later Mrs. Houston applied for a divorce, which in those days had to be granted by the state legislature. Inevitably reports derogatory to her had got abroad. Almost the first tidings of Governor Houston's whereabouts were contained in a letter he wrote from somewhere in the Indian country to my father, a member of the legislature to whom Mrs. Houston had applied, in which he said that these reports had come to his ears. "They are," he wrote, "as false as hell. If they be not stopped I will return to Tennessee and have the heart's blood of him who repeats them. A nobler, purer woman never lived. She should be promptly given the divorce she asks. I alone am to blame."

She married again, though not the lover she had discarded. I knew her in her old age—a gentle, placid lady, in whose face I used to fancy I could read lines of sorrow and regret. He, to close this chapter, likewise married again a wise and womanly woman who bore him many children and with whom he lived happy ever after. Meanwhile, however, he had dwelt with the Indians and had become an Indian chief. "Big Drunk, they called me," he said to his familiars. His enemies averred that he brought into the world a whole tribe of half-breeds.

II

Houston was a rare performer before a popular audience. His speech abounded with argumentative appeal and bristled with illustrative anecdote, and, when occasion required, with apt repartee.

Once an Irishman in the crowd bawled out, "ye were goin' to sell
Texas to
England."

Houston paused long enough to center attention upon the quibble and then said: "My friend, I first tried, unsuccessfully, to have the United States take Texas as a gift. Not until I threatened to turn Texas over to England did I finally succeed. There may be within the sound of my voice some who have knowledge of sheep culture. They have doubtless seen a motherless lamb put to the breast of a cross old ewe who refused it suck. Then the wise shepherd calls his dog and there is no further trouble. My friend, England was my dog."

He was inveighing against the New York Tribune. Having described Horace Greeley as the sum of all villainy—"whose hair is white, whose skin is white, whose eyes are white, whose clothes are white, and whose liver is in my opinion of the same color"—he continued: "The assistant editor of the Try-bune is Robinson—Solon

Robinson. He is an Irishman, an Orange Irishman, a redhaired Irishman!" Casting his eye over the audience and seeing quite a sprinkling of redheads, and realizing that he had perpetrated a slip of tongue, he added: "Fellow citizens, when I say that Robinson is a red-haired Irishman I mean no disrespect to persons whose hair is of that color. I have been a close observer of men and women for thirty years, and I never knew a red-haired man who was not an honest man, nor a red-headed woman who was not a virtuous woman; and I give it you as my candid opinion that had it not been for Robinson's red hair he would have been hanged long ago."

His pathos was not far behind his humor—though he used it sparingly. At a certain town in Texas there lived a desperado who had threatened to kill him on sight. The town was not on the route of his speaking dates but he went out of his way to include it. A great concourse assembled to hear him. He spoke in the open air and, as he began, observed his man leaning against a tree armed to the teeth and waiting for him to finish. After a few opening remarks, he dropped into the reminiscential. He talked of the old times in Texas. He told in thrilling terms of the Alamo and of Goliad. There was not a dry eye in earshot. Then he grew personal.

"I see Tom Gilligan over yonder. A braver man never lived than Tom
Gilligan. He fought by my side at San Jacinto. Together we buried poor Bill
Holman. But for his skill and courage I should not be here to-day. He—"

There was a stir in front. Gilligan had thrown away his knife and gun and was rushing unarmed through the crowd, tears streaming down his face.

"For God's sake, Houston," he cried, "don't say another word and forgive me my cowardly intention."

From that time to his death Tom Gilligan was Houston's devoted friend.

General Houston voted against the Kansas-Nebraska Bill, and as a consequence lost his seat in the Senate. It was thought, and freely said, that for good and all he was down and out. He went home and announced himself a candidate for governor of Texas.

The campaign that followed was of unexampled bitterness. The secession wave was already mounting high. Houston was an uncompromising Unionist. His defeat was generally expected. But there was no beating such a man in a fair and square contest before the people. When the votes were counted he led his competitor by a big majority. As governor he refused two years later to sign the ordinance of secession and was deposed from office by force. He died before the end of the war which so signally vindicated his wisdom and verified his forecast.

III

Stephen Arnold Douglas was the Charles James Fox of American politics. He was not a gambler as Fox was. But he went the other gaits and was possessed of a sweetness of disposition which made him, like Fox, loved where he was personally known. No one could resist the *bonhomie* of Douglas.

They are not all Puritans in New England. Catch a Yankee off his base, quite away from home, and he can be as gay as anybody. Boston and Charleston were in high party times nearest alike of any two American cities.

Douglas was a Green Mountain boy. He was born in Vermont. As Seargent Prentiss had done he migrated beyond the Alleghanies before he came of age, settling in Illinois as Prentiss had settled in Mississippi, to grow into a typical Westerner as Prentiss into a typical Southerner.

There was never a more absurd theory than that, begot of sectional aims and the sectional spirit, which proposed a geographic alignment of Cavalier and Puritan. When sectionalism had brought a kindred people to blows over the institution of African slavery there were Puritans who fought on the Southern side and Cavaliers who fought on the Northern side. What was Stonewall Jackson but a Puritan? What were Custer, Stoneman and Kearny but Cavaliers? Wadsworth was as absolute an aristocrat as Hampton.

In the old days before the war of sections the South was full of typical Southerners of Northern birth. John A. Quitman, who went from New York, and Robert J. Walker, who went from Pennsylvania to Mississippi; James H. Hammond, whose father, a teacher, went from Massachusetts to South Carolina. John Slidell, born and bred in New York, was thirty years old when he went to Louisiana. Albert Sidney Johnston, the rose and expectancy of the young Confederacy—the most typical of rebel soldiers—had not a drop of Southern blood in his veins, born in Kentucky a few months after his father and mother had arrived there from Connecticut. The list might be extended indefinitely.

Climate, which has something to do with temperament, has not so much to do with character as is often imagined. All of us are more or less the creatures of environment. In the South after a fashion the duello flourished. Because it had not flourished in the North there rose a notion that the Northerners would not fight. It proved to those who thought it a costly mistake.

Down to the actual secession of 1860-61 the issue of issues—the issue behind all issues—was the preservation of the Union. Between 1820 and 1850, by a series of compromises, largely the work of Mr. Clay, its threatened disruption had been averted. The Kansas-Nebraska Bill put a sore strain upon conservative elements North and South. The Whig Party went to pieces. Mr. Clay passed from the scene. Had he lived until the presidential election of 1852 he would have given his support to Franklin Pierce, as Daniel Webster did. Mr. Buchanan was not a General Jackson. Judge Douglas, who sought to play the rôle of Mr. Clay, was too late. The secession leaders held the whip hand in the Gulf States. South Carolina was to have her will at last. Crash came the shot in Charleston Harbor and the fall of Sumter. Curiously enough two persons of Kentucky birth—Abraham Lincoln and Jefferson Davis—led the rival hosts of war into which an untenable and indefensible system of slave labor, for which the two sections were equally responsible, had precipitated an unwilling people.

Had Judge Douglas lived he would have been Mr. Lincoln's main reliance in Congress. As a debater his resources and prowess were rarely equaled and never surpassed. His personality, whether in debate or private conversation, was attractive in the highest degree. He possessed a full, melodious voice, convincing fervor and ready wit.

He had married for his second wife the reigning belle of the National Capital, a great-niece of Mrs. Madison, whose very natural ambitions quickened and spurred his own.

It was fated otherwise. Like Clay, Webster, Calhoun and Blaine he was to be denied the Presidency. The White House was barred to him. He was not yet fifty when he died.

Tidings of his death took the country by surprise. But already the sectional battle was on and it produced only a momentary impression, to be soon forgotten amid the overwhelming tumult of events. He has lain in his grave now nearly sixty years. Upon the legislation of his time his name was writ first in water and then in blood. He received less than his desert in life and the historic record has scarcely done justice to his merit. He was as great a party leader as Clay. He could hold his own in debate with Webster and Calhoun. He died a very poor man, though his opportunity for enrichment by perfectly legitimate means were many. It is enough to say that he lacked the business instinct and set no value upon money; scrupulously upright in his official dealing; holding his senatorial duties above all price and beyond the suspicion of dirt.

Touching a matter which involved a certain outlay in the winter of 1861, he laughingly said to me: "I haven't the wherewithal to pay for a bottle of whisky and shall have to borrow of Arnold Harris the wherewithal to take me home."

His wife was a glorious creature. Early one morning calling at their home to see Judge Douglas I was ushered into the library, where she was engaged setting things to rights. My entrance took her by surprise. I had often seen her in full ballroom regalia and in becoming out-of-door costume, but as, in gingham gown and white apron, she turned, a little startled by my sudden appearance, smiles and blushes in spite of herself, I thought I had never seen any woman so beautiful before. She married again — the lover whom gossip said she had thrown over to marry Judge Douglas—and the story went that her second marriage was not very happy.

IV

In the midsummer of 1859 the burning question among the newsmen of Washington was the Central American Mission. England and France had displayed activity in that quarter and it was deemed important that the United States should sit up and take notice. An Isthmian canal was being considered.

Speculation was rife whom Mr. Buchanan would send to represent us. The press gang of the National Capital was all at sea. There was scarcely a Democratic leader of national prominence whose name was not mentioned in that connection, though speculation from day to day eddied round Mr. James S. Rollins, of Missouri, an especial friend of the President and a most accomplished public man.

At the height of excitement I happened to be in the library of the State Department. I was on a step-ladder in quest of a book when I heard a messenger say to the librarian: "The President is in the Secretary's room and wants to have Mr. Dimitry come there right away." An inspiration shot through me like a flash. They had chosen Alexander Dimitry for the Central American Mission.

He was the official translator of the Department of State. Though an able and learned man he was not in the line of preferment. He was without political standing or backing of any sort. At first blush a more unlikely, impossible appointment could hardly be suggested. But—so on the instant I reasoned—he was peculiarly fitted in his own person for the post in question. Though of Greek origin he looked like a Spaniard. He spoke the Spanish language fluently. He had the procedure of the State Department at his finger's ends. He was the head of a charming domestic fabric—his daughters the prettiest girls in Washington. Why not?

I climbed down from my stepladder and made tracks for the office of the afternoon newspaper for which I was doing all-round work. I was barely on time, the last forms being locked when I got there. I had the editorial page opened and inserted at the top of the leading column a double-leaded paragraph announcing that the agony was over—that the Gordian knot was cut—that Alexander Dimitry had been selected as Envoy Extraordinary and Minister Plenipotentiary to the Central American States.

It proved a veritable sensation as well as a notable scoop. To increase my glory the correspondents of the New York dailies scouted it. But in a day or two it was officially confirmed. General Cass, the Secretary of State, sent for me, having learned that I had been in the department about the time of the consultation between the President, himself and Mr. Dimitry.

"How did you get this?" he asked rather sharply.

"Out of my inner consciousness," I answered with flippant familiarity.
"Didn't you know that I have what they call second sight?"

The old gentleman laughed amiably. "It would seem so," he said, and sent me about my business without further inquiry.

V

In the National Capital the winter of 1860-61 was both stormy and nebulous. Parties were at sea. The Northerners in Congress had learned the trick of bullying from the Southerners. In the Senate, Chandler was a match for Toombs; and in the House, Thaddeus Stevens for Keitt and Lamar. All of them, more or less, were playing a game. If sectional war, which was incessantly threatened by the two extremes, had been keenly realized and seriously considered it might have been averted. Very few believed that it would come to actual war.

A convention of Border State men, over which ex-President John Tyler presided, was held in Washington. It might as well have been held at the North Pole. Moderate men were brushed aside, their counsels whistled down the wind. There was a group of Senators, headed by Wigfall of Texas, who meant disunion and war, and another group, headed by Seward, Hale and Chase, who had been goaded up to this. Reading contemporary history and, seeing the high-mightiness with which the Germans began what we conceive their raid upon humanity, we are wont to regard it as evidence of incredible stupidity, whereas it was, in point of fact, rather a miscalculation of forces. That was the error of the secession leaders. They refused to count the cost. Yancey firmly believed that England would be forced to intervene. The mills of Lancashire he thought could not get on without Southern cotton. He was sent abroad. He found Europe solid against slavery and therefore set against the Confederacy. He came home with what is called a broken heart—the dreams of a lifetime shattered—and, in a kind of dazed stupor, laid himself down to die. With Richmond in flames and the exultant shouts of the detested yet victorious Yankees in his ears, he did die.

Wigfall survived but a few years. He was less a dreamer than Yancey. A man big of brain and warm of heart he had gone from the ironclad provincialism of South Carolina to the windswept vagaries of Texas. He believed wholly the Yancey confession of faith; that secession was a constitutional right; that African slavery was ordained of God; that the South was paramount, the North inferior. Yet in worldly knowledge he had learned more than Yancey—was an abler man than Jefferson Davis—and but for his affections and generous habits he would have made a larger figure in the war, having led the South's exit from the Senate.

VI

I do not think that either Hammond or Chestnut, the Senators from South Carolina, both men of parts, had at bottom much belief in the practicability of the Confederate movement. Neither had the

Senators from Arkansas and Alabama, nor Brown, of Mississippi, the colleague of Jefferson Davis. Mason, of Virginia, a dogged old donkey, and Iverson, of Georgia, another, were the kind of men whom Wigfall dominated.

One of the least confident of those who looked on and afterward fell in line was the Vice President, John C. Breckenridge, of Kentucky. He was the Beau Sabreur among statesmen as Albert Sidney Johnston, among soldiers. Never man handsomer in person or more winning in manners. Sprung from a race of political aristocrats, he was born to early and shining success in public life. Of moderate opinions, winning and prudent, wherever he appeared he carried his audience with him. He had been elected on the ticket with Buchanan to the second office under the Government, when he was but five and thirty years of age. There was nothing for him to gain from a division of the Union; the Presidency, perhaps, if the Union continued undivided. But he could not resist the onrush of disunionism, went with the South, which he served first in the field and later as Confederate Secretary of War, and after a few years of self-imposed exile in Europe returned to Kentucky to die at four and fifty, a defeated and disappointed old man.

The adjoining state of Tennessee was represented in the Senate by one of the most problematic characters in American history. With my father, who remained his friend through life, he had entered the state legislature in 1835, and having served ten years in the lower House of Congress, and four years as governor of Tennessee he came back in 1857 to the National Capital, a member of the Upper House. He was Andrew Johnson.

I knew him from my childhood. Thrice that I can recall I saw him weep; never did I see him laugh. Life had been very serious, albeit very successful, to him. Of unknown parentage, the wife he had married before he was one and twenty had taught him to read. Yet at six and twenty he was in the Tennessee General Assembly and at four and thirty in Congress.

There was from first to last not a little about him to baffle conjecture. I should call him a cross between Jack Cade and Aaron Burr. His sympathies were easily stirred by rags in distress. But he was uncompromising in his detestation of the rich. It was said that he hated "a biled shirt." He would have nothing to do "with people who wore broadcloth," though he carefully dressed himself. When, as governor of Tennessee, he came to Nashville he refused many invitations to take his first New Year's dinner with a party of toughs at the house of a river roustabout.

There was nothing of the tough about him, however. His language was careful and exact. I never heard him utter an oath or tell a risqué story. He passed quite fifteen years in Washington, a total abstainer from the use of intoxicants. He fell into the occasional-drink habit during the dark days of the War. But after some costly experience he dropped it and continued a total abstainer to the end of his days.

He had, indeed, admirable self-control. I do not believe a more conscientious man ever lived. His judgments were sometimes peculiar, but they were upright and sincere, having reasons, which he could give with power and effect, behind them. Yet was he a born politician, crafty to a degree, and always successful, relying upon a popular following which never failed him.

In 1860 he supported the quasi-secession Breckenridge and Lane Presidential ticket, but in 1861 he stood true to the Union, retaining his seat in the Senate until he was appointed military governor of Tennessee. Nominated for Vice President on the ticket with Lincoln, in 1864, he was elected, and upon the assassination of Lincoln succeeded to the Presidency. Having served out his term as President he returned to Tennessee to engage in the hottest kind of politics, and though at the outset defeated finally regained his seat in the Senate of the United States.

He hated Grant with a holy hate. His first act on reëntering the Senate was to deliver an implacably bitter speech against the President. It was his last public appearance. He went thence to his home in East Tennessee, gratified and happy, to die in a few weeks.

VII

There used to be a story about Raleigh, in North Carolina, where Andrew Johnson was born, which whispered that he was a natural son of William Ruffin, an eminent jurist in the earlier years of the nineteenth century. It was analogous to the story that Lincoln was the natural son of various paternities from time to time assigned to him. I had my share in running that calumny to cover. It was a lie out of whole cloth with nothing whatever to support or excuse it. I reached the bottom of it to discover proof of its baselessness abundant and conclusive. In Johnson's case I take it that the story had nothing other to rest on than the obscurity of his birth and the quality of his talents. Late in life Johnson went to Raleigh and caused to be erected a modest tablet over the spot pointed out as the grave of his progenitor, saying, I was told by persons claiming to have been present, "I place this stone over the last earthly abode of my alleged father."

Johnson, in the saying of the countryside, "out-married himself." His wife was a plain woman, but came of good family. One day, when a child, so the legend ran, she saw passing through the Greenville street in which her people lived, a woman, a boy and a cow, the boy carrying a pack over his shoulder. They were obviously weary and hungry. Extreme poverty could present no sadder picture. "Mother," cried the girl, "there goes the man I am going to marry." She was thought to be in jest. But a few years later she made her banter good and lived to see her husband President of the United States and with him to occupy the White House at Washington.

Much has been written of the humble birth and iron fortune of Abraham Lincoln. He had no such obstacles to overcome as either Andrew Jackson or Andrew Johnson. Jackson, a prisoner of war, was liberated, a lad of sixteen, from the British pen at Charleston, without a relative, a friend or a dollar in the world, having to make his way upward through the most aristocratic community of the country and the time. Johnson, equally friendless and penniless, started as a poor tailor in a rustic village. Lincoln must therefore, take third place among our self-made Presidents. The Hanks family were not paupers. He had a wise and helpful stepmother. He was scarcely worse off than most young fellows of his neighborhood, first in Indiana and then in Illinois. On this side justice has never been rendered to Jackson and Johnson. In the case of Jackson the circumstance was forgotten, while Johnson too often dwelt upon it and made capital out of it.

Under date of the 23rd of May, 1919, the Hon. Josephus Daniels, Secretary of the Navy, writes me the following letter, which I violate no confidence in reproducing in this connection:

MY DEAR MARSE HENRY:—

I can't tell you how much delight and pleasure your reminiscences in the Saturday Evening Post have given me, as well as the many others who have followed them, and I suppose you will put them in a volume when they are finished, so that we may have the pleasure of reading them in connected order.

As you know, I live in Raleigh and I was very much interested in your article in the issue of April 5, 1919, with reference to Andrew Johnson, in which you quote a story that "used to be current in Raleigh, that he was the son of William Ruffin, an eminent jurist of the ninetenth century." I had never heard this story, but the story that was gossiped there was that he was the son of a certain Senator Haywood. I ran that story down and found that it had no foundation whatever, because if he had been the son of the Senator reputed to be his father, the Senator was of the age of twelve years when Andrew Johnson was born.

My own information is, for I have made some investigation of it, that the story about Andrew Johnson's having a father other than the husband of his mother, is as wanting in foundation as the story about Abraham Lincoln. You did a great service in running that down and exposing it, and I trust before you finish your book that you will make further investigation and be able to do a like service in repudiating the unjust, idle gossip with reference to Andrew Johnson. In your article you say that persons who claim to have been present when Johnson came to Raleigh and erected a monument over the grave of his father, declare that Johnson said he placed this stone over the last earthly abode of "my alleged father."

That is one phase of the gossip, and the other is that he said "my reputed father," both equally false.

The late Mr. Pulaski Cowper, who was private secretary to Governor Bragg, of our State, just prior to the war, and who was afterwards president of our leading life insurance company, a gentleman of high character, and of the best memory, was present at the time that Johnson made the address from which you quote the rumor. Mr. Cowper wrote an article for The News and Observer, giving the story and relating that Johnson said that "he was glad to come to Raleigh to erect a tablet to his father." The truth is that while his father was a man of little or no education, he held the position of janitor at the State Capitol, and he was not wanting in qualities which made him superior to his humble position. If he had been living in this day he would have been given a lifesaving medal, for upon the occasion of a picnic near Raleigh when the cry came that children were drowning he was the first to leap in and endanger his life to save them.

Andrew Johnson's mother was related to the Chappell family, of which there are a number of citizens of standing and character near Raleigh, several of them having been ministers of the Gospel, and one at least having gained distinction as a missionary in China.

I am writing you because I know that your story will be read and accepted and I thought you would be glad to have this story, based upon a study and investigation and personal knowledge of Mr. Cowper, whose character and competency are well known in North Carolina.

Chapter the Seventh

An Old Newspaper Rookery—Reactionary Sectionalism in Cincinnati and
Louisville—*The Courier-Journal*

I

My dream of wealth through my commission on the Confederate cotton I was to sell to English buyers was quickly shattered. The cotton was burned and I found myself in the early spring of 1865 in the little village of Glendale, a suburb of Cincinnati, where the future Justice Stanley Matthews had his home. His wife was a younger sister of my mother. My grandmother was still alive and lived with her daughter and son-in-law.

I was received with open arms. A few days later the dear old lady said to me: "I suppose, my son, you are rather a picked bird after your adventures in the South. You certainly need better clothing. I have some money in bank and it is freely yours."

I knew that my Uncle Stanley had put her up to this, and out of sheer curiosity I asked her how much she could let me have. She named what seemed to me a stupendous sum. I thanked her, told her I had quite a sufficiency for the time being, slipped into town and pawned my watch; that is, as I made light of it afterward in order to escape the humiliation of borrowing from an uncle whose politics I did not approve, I went with my collateral to an uncle who had no politics at all and got fifty dollars on it! Before the money was gone I had found, through Judge Matthews, congenial work.

There was in Cincinnati but one afternoon newspaper—the Evening Times—owned by Calvin W. Starbuck. He had been a practical printer but was grown very rich. He received me kindly, said the editorial force was quite full—must always be, on a daily newspaper—"but," he added, "my brother, Alexander Starbuck, who has been running the amusements, wants to go a-fishing in Canada—to be gone a month—and, if you wish, you can during his absence sub for him."

It was just to my hand and liking. Before Alexander Starbuck returned the leading editor of the paper fell from a ferryboat crossing the Ohio River and was drowned. The next day General Starbuck sent for me and offered me the vacant place.

"Why, general," I said, "I am an outlawed man: I do not agree with your politics. I do not see how I can undertake a place so conspicuous and responsible."

He replied: "I propose to engage you as an editorial manager. It is as if building a house you should be head carpenter, I the architect. The difference in salary will be seventy-five dollars a week against fifteen dollars a week."

I took the place.

II

The office of the Evening Times was a queer old curiosity shop. I set to and turned it inside out. I had very pronounced journalistic notions of my own and applied them in every department of the sleepy old money-maker. One afternoon a week later I put forth a paper whose oldest reader could not have recognized it. The next morning's Cincinnati Commercial contained a flock of paragraphs to which the Chattanooga-Cincinnati-Rebel Evening Times furnished the keynote.

They made funny reading, but they threw a dangerous flare upon my "past" and put me at a serious disadvantage. It happened that when Artemus Ward had been in town a fortnight before he gave me a dinner and had some of his friends to meet me. Among these was a young fellow of the name of Halstead, who, I was told, was the coming man on the Commercial.

Round to the Commercial office I sped, and being conducted to this person, who received me very blandly, I said: "Mr. Halstead, I am a journeyman day laborer in your city—the merest bird of passage, with my watch at the pawnbroker's. As soon as I am able to get out of town I mean to go—and I came to ask if you can think the personal allusions to me in to-day's paper, which may lose me my job but can nowise hurt the Times, are quite fair—even—since I am without defense—quite manly."

He looked at me with that quizzical, serio-comic stare which so became him, and with great heartiness replied: "No—they were damned mean—though I did not realize how mean. The mark was so obvious and tempting I could not resist, but—there shall be no more of them. Come, let us go and have a drink."

That was the beginning of a friendship which brought happiness to both of us and lasted nearly half a century, to the hour of his death, when, going from Louisville to Cincinnati, I helped to lay him away in Spring Grove Cemetery.

I had no thought of remaining in Cincinnati. My objective was Nashville, where the young woman who was to become my wife, and whom I had not seen for nearly two years, was living with her family. During the summer Mr. Francisco, the business manager of the Evening Times, had a scheme to buy the Toledo Commercial, in conjunction with Mr. Comly, of Columbus, and to engage me as editor conjointly with Mr. Harrison Gray Otis as publisher. It looked very good. Toledo threatened Cleveland and Detroit as a lake port. But nothing could divert me. As soon as Parson Brownlow, who was governor of Tennessee and making things lively for the returning rebels, would allow, I was going to Nashville.

About the time the way was cleared my two pals, or bunkies, of the Confederacy, Albert Roberts and George Purvis, friends from boyhood, put in an appearance. They were on their way to the capital of Tennessee. The father of Albert Roberts was chief owner of the Republican Banner, an old and highly respectable newspaper, which had for nearly four years lain in a state of suspension. Their plan now was to revive its publication, Purvis to be business manager, and Albert and I to be editors. We had no cash. Nobody on our side of the line had any cash. But John Roberts owned a farm he could mortgage for money enough to start us. What had I to say?

Less than a week later saw us back at home winnowing the town for subscribers and advertising. We divided it into districts, each taking a specified territory. The way we boys hustled was a sight to see. But the way the community warmed to us was another. When the familiar headline, The Republican Banner, made its apearance there was a popular hallelujah, albeit there were five other dailies ahead of us. A year later there was only one, and it was nowise a competitor.

Albert Roberts had left his girl, Edith Scott, the niece of Huxley, whom I have before mentioned, in Montgomery, Alabama. Purvis' girl, Sophie Searcy, was in Selma. Their hope was to have enough money by Christmas each to pay a visit to those distant places. My girl was on the spot, and we had resolved, money or no money, to be married without delay. Before New Year's the three of us were wedded and comfortably settled, with funds galore, for the paper had thrived consumingly. It had thrived so consumingly that after a little I was able to achieve the wish of my heart and to go to London, taking my wife and my "great American novel" with me. I have related elsewhere what came of this and what happened to me.

III

That bread cast upon the waters—"'dough' put out at usance," as Joseph Jefferson used to phrase it—shall return after many days has been I dare say discovered by most persons who have perpetrated acts of kindness, conscious or unconscious. There was a poor, broken-down English actor with a passion for Chaucer, whom I was wont to encounter in the Library of Congress. His voice was quite gone. Now and again I had him join me in a square meal. Once in a while I paid his room rent. I was loath to leave him when the break came in 1861, though he declared he had "expectations," and made sure he would not starve.

I was passing through Regent Street in London, when a smart brougham drove up to the curb and a wheezy voice called after me. It was my old friend, Newton. His "expectations" had not failed him, he had come into a property and was living in affluence.

He knew London as only a Bohemian native and to the manner born could know it. His sense of bygone obligation knew no bounds. Between him and John Mahoney and Artemus Ward I was made at home in what might be called the mysteries and eccentricities of differing phases of life in the British metropolis not commonly accessible to the foreign casual. In many after visits this familiar knowledge has served me well. But Newton did not live to know of some good fortune that came to me and to feel my gratitude to him, as dear old John Mahoney did. When I was next in London he was gone.

It was not, however, the actor, Newton, whom I had in mind in offering a bread-upon-the-water moral, but a certain John Hatcher, the memory of whom in my case illustrates it much better. He was a wit and a poet. He had been State Librarian of Tennessee. Nothing could keep him out of the service, though he was a sad cripple and wholly unequal to its requirements. He fell ill. I had the opportunity to care for him. When the war was over his old friend, George D.

Prentice, called him to Louisville to take an editorial place on the Journal.

About the same time Mr. Walter Haldeman returned from the South and resumed the suspended publication of the Louisville Courier. He was in the prime of life, a man of surpassing energy, enterprise and industry, and had with him the popular sympathy. Mr. Prentice was nearly three score and ten. The stream had passed him by. The Journal was not only beginning to feel the strain but was losing ground. In this emergency Hatcher came to the rescue. I was just back from London and was doing noticeable work on the Nashville Banner.

"Here is your man," said Hatcher to Mr. Prentice and Mr. Henderson, the owners of the Journal; and I was invited to come to Louisville.

After I had looked over the field and inspected the Journal's books I was satisfied that a union with the Courier was the wisest solution of the newspaper situation, and told them so. Meanwhile Mr. Haldeman, whom I had known in the Confederacy, sent for me. He offered me the same terms for part ownership and sole editorship of the Courier, which the Journal people had offered me. This I could not accept, but proposed as an alternative the consolidation of the two on an equal basis. He was willing enough for the consolidation, but not on equal terms. There was nothing for it but a fight. I took the Journal and began to hammer the Courier.

A dead summer was before us, but Mr. Henderson had plenty of money and was willing to spend it. During the contest not an unkind word was printed on either side. After stripping the Journal to its heels it had very little to go on or to show for what had once been a prosperous business. But circulation flowed in. From eighteen hundred daily it quickly mounted to ten thousand; from fifteen hundred weekly to fifty thousand. The middle of October it looked as if we had a straight road before us.

But I knew better. I had discovered that the field, no matter how worked, was not big enough to support two rival dailies. There was toward the last of October on the edge of town a real-estate sale which Mr. Haldeman and I attended. Here was my chance for a play. I must have bid up to a hundred thousand dollars and did actually buy nearly ten thousand dollars of the lots put up at auction, relying upon some money presently coming to my wife.

I could see that it made an impression on Mr. Haldeman. Returning in the carriage which had brought us out I said: "Mr. Haldeman, I am going to ruin you. But I am going to run up a money obligation to Isham Henderson I shall never be able to discharge. You need an editor. I need a publisher. Let us put these two newspapers together, buy the Democrat, and, instead of cutting one another's throats, go after Cincinnati and St. Louis. You will recall that I proposed this to you in the beginning. What is the matter with it now?"

Nothing was the matter with it. He agreed at once. The details were soon adjusted. Ten days later there appeared upon the doorsteps of the city in place of the three familiar visitors, a double-headed stranger, calling itself the Courier-Journal. Our exclusive possession of the field thus acquired lasted two years. At the end of these we found that at least the appearance of competition was indispensable and willingly acepted an offer from a proposed Republican organ for a division of the Press dispatches which we controlled. Then and there the real prosperity of the Courier-Journal began, the paper having made no money out of its monopoly.

IV

Reconstruction, as it was called — ruin were a fitter name for it — had just begun. The South was imprisoned, awaiting the executioner. The Constitution of the United States hung in the balance. The Federal Union faced the threat of sectional despotism. The spirit of the time was martial law. The gospel of proscription ruled in Congress. Radicalism, vitalized by the murder of Abraham Lincoln and inflamed by the inadequate effort of Andrew Johnson to carry out the policies of Lincoln, was in the saddle riding furiously toward a carpetbag Poland and a negroized Ireland.

The Democratic Party, which, had it been stronger, might have interposed, lay helpless. It, too, was crushed to earth. Even the Border

States, which had not been embraced by the military agencies and federalized machinery erected over the Gulf States, were seriously menaced. Never did newspaper enterprise set out under gloomier auspices.

There was a party of reaction in Kentucky, claiming to be Democratic, playing to the lead of the party of repression at the North. It refused to admit that the head of the South was in the lion's mouth and that the first essential was to get it out. The Courier-Journal proposed to stroke the mane, not twist the tail of the lion. Thus it stood between two fires. There arose a not unnatural distrust of the journalistic monopoly created by the consolidation of the three former dailies into a single newspaper, carrying an unfamiliar hyphenated headline. Touching its policy of sectional conciliation it picked its way perilously through the cross currents of public opinion. There was scarcely a sinister purpose that was not alleged against it by its enemies; scarcely a hostile device that was not undertaken to put it down and drive it out.

Its constituency represented an unknown quantity. In any event it had to be created. Meanwhile, it must rely upon its own resources, sustained by the courage of the venture, by the integrity of its convictions and aims, and by faith in the future of the city, the state and the country.

Still, to be precise, it was the morning of Sunday, November 8,1868. The night before the good people of Louisville had gone to bed expecting nothing unusual to happen. They awoke to encounter an uninvited guest arrived a little before the dawn. No hint of its coming had got abroad; and thus the surprise was the greater. Truth to say, it was not a pleased surprise, because, as it flared before the eye of the startled citizen in big Gothic letters, The Courier-Journal, there issued thence an aggressive self-confidence which affronted the *amour propre* of the sleepy villagers. They were used to a very different style of newspaper approach.

Nor was the absence of a timorous demeanor its only offense. The Courier had its partisans, the Journal and the Democrat had their friends. The trio stood as ancient landmarks, as recognized and familiar institutions. Here was a double-headed monster which, without saying "by your leave" or "blast your eyes" or any other politeness, had taken possession of each man's doorstep, looking very like it had brought its knitting and was come to stay.

The Journal established by Mr. Prentice, the Courier by Mr. Haldeman and the Democrat by Mr. Harney, had been according to the standards of those days successful newspapers. But the War of Sections had made many changes. At its close new conditions appeared on every side. A revolution had come into the business and the spirit of American journalism.

In Louisville three daily newspapers had for a generation struggled for the right of way. Yet Louisville was a city of the tenth or twelfth class, having hardly enough patronage to sustain one daily newspaper of the first or second class. The idea of consolidating the three thus contending to divide a patronage so insufficient, naturally suggested itself during the years immediately succeeding the war. But it did not take definite shape until 1868.

Mr. Haldeman had returned from a somewhat picturesque and not altogether profitable pursuit of his "rights in the territories" and had resumed the suspended publication of the Courier with encouraging prospects. I had succeeded Mr. Prentice in the editorship and part ownership of the Journal. Both Mr. Haldeman and I were newspaper men to the manner born and bred; old and good friends; and after our rivalry of six months maintained with activity on both sides, but without the publication of an unkind word on either, a union of forces seemed exigent. To practical men the need of this was not a debatable question. All that was required was an adjustment of the details. Beginning with the simple project of joining the Courier and the Journal, it ended by the purchase of the Democrat, which it did not seem safe to leave outside.

V

The political conditions in Kentucky were anomalous. The Republican Party had not yet definitely taken root. Many of the rich old Whigs, who had held to the Government — to save their slaves —

resenting Lincoln's Emancipation Proclamation, had turned Democrats. Most of the before-the-war Democrats had gone with the Confederacy. The party in power called itself Democratic, but was in fact a body of reactionary nondescripts claiming to be Unionists and clinging, or pretending to cling, to the hard-and-fast prejudices of other days.

The situation may be the better understood when I add that "negro testimony"—the introduction to the courts of law of the newly made freedmen as witnesses—barred by the state constitution, was the burning issue. A murder committed in the presence of a thousand negroes could not be lawfully proved in court. Everything from a toothbrush to a cake of soap might be cited before a jury, but not a human being if his skin happened to be black.

[Illustration: Mr. Watterson's Editorial Staff in 1868, When the Three Daily Newspapers of Louisville Were United into the *Courier-Journal*." Mr. George D. Prentice and Mr. Watterson Are in the Center.]

To my mind this was monstrous. From my cradle I had detested slavery. The North will never know how many people at the South did so. I could not go with the Republican Party, however, because after the death of Abraham Lincoln it had intrenched itself in the proscription of Southern men. The attempt to form a third party had shown no strength and had broken down. There was nothing for me, and the Confederates who were with me, but the ancient label of a Democracy worn by a riffraff of opportunists, Jeffersonian principles having quite gone to seed. But I proposed to lead and reform it, not to follow and fall in behind the selfish and short-sighted time servers who thought the people had learned nothing and forgot nothing; and instant upon finding myself in the saddle I sought to ride down the mass of ignorance which was at least for the time being mainly what I had to look to for a constituency.

Mr. Prentice, who knew the lay of the ground better than I did, advised against it. The personal risk counted for something. Very early in the action I made a direct fighting issue, which—the combat interdicted—gave me the opportunity to declare—with something of the bully in the tone—that I might not be able to hit a barn door at ten paces, but could shoot with any man in Kentucky across a pocket handkerchief, holding myself at all times answerable and accessible. I had a fairly good fighting record in the army and it was not doubted that I meant what I said.

But it proved a bitter, hard, uphill struggle, for a long while against odds, before negro testimony was carried. A generation of politicians were sent to the rear. Finally, in 1876, a Democratic State Convention put its mark upon me as a Democrat by appointing me a Delegate at large to the National Democratic Convention of that year called to meet at St. Louis to put a Presidential ticket in the field.

The Courier-Journal having come to represent all three of the English dailies of the city the public began to rebel. It could not see that instead of three newspapers of the third or fourth class Louisville was given one newspaper of the first class; that instead of dividing the local patronage in three inadequate portions, wasted upon a triple competition, this patronage was combined, enabling the one newspaper to engage in a more equal competition with the newspapers of such rival and larger cities as Cincinnati and St. Louis; and that one of the contracting parties needing an editor, the other a publisher, in coming together the two were able to put their trained faculties to the best account.

Nevertheless, during thirty-five years Mr. Haldeman and I labored side by side, not the least difference having arisen between us. The attacks to which we were subjected from time to time drew us together the closer. These attacks were sometimes irritating and sometimes comical, but they had one characteristic feature: Each started out apparently under a high state of excitement. Each seemed to have some profound cause of grief, to be animated by implacable hate and to aim at nothing short of annihilation. Frequently the assailants would lie in wait to see how the Courier-Journal's cat was going to jump, in order that they might take the other side; and invariably, even if the Courier-Journal stood for the reforms they affected to stand for, they began a system of misrepresentation and abuse. In no instance did they attain any success.

Only once, during the Free Silver craze of 1896, and the dark and tragic days that followed it the three or four succeeding years, the paper having stood, as it had stood during the Greenback craze, for sound money, was the property in danger. It cost more of labor and patience to save it from destruction than it had cost to create it thirty years before. Happily Mr. Haldeman lived to see the rescue complete, the tide turned and the future safe.

VI

A newspaper, like a woman, must not only be honest, but must seem to be honest; acts of levity, loose unbecoming expressions or behavior—though never so innocent—tending in the one and in the other to lower reputation and discredit character. During my career I have proceeded under a confident belief in this principle of newspaper ethics and an unfailing recognition of its mandates. I truly believe that next after business integrity in newspaper management comes disinterestedness in the public service, and next after disinterestedness come moderation and intelligence, cleanliness and good feeling, in dealing with affairs and its readers.

From that blessed Sunday morning, November 8, 1868, to this good day, I have known no other life and had no other aim. Those were indeed parlous times. It was an era of transition. Upon the field of battle, after four years of deadly but unequal combat, the North had vanquished the South. The victor stood like a giant, with blood aflame, eyes dilate and hands uplifted again to strike. The victim lay prostrate. Save self-respect and manhood all was lost. Clasping its memories to its bosom the South sank helpless amid the wreck of its fortunes, whilst the North, the benign influence of the great Lincoln withdrawn, proceeded to decide its fate. To this ghastly end had come slavery and secession, and all the pomp, pride and circumstance of the Confederacy. To this bitter end had come the soldiership of Lee and Jackson and Johnston and the myriads of brave men who followed them.

The single Constitutional barrier that had stood between the people of the stricken section and political extinction was about to be removed by the exit of Andrew Johnson from the White House. In his place a man of blood and iron—for such was the estimate at that time placed upon Grant—had been elected President. The Republicans in Congress, checked for a time by Johnson, were at length to have entire sway under Thaddeus Stevens. Reconstruction was to be thorough and merciless. To meet these conditions was the first requirement of the Courier-Journal, a newspaper conducted by outlawed rebels and published on the sectional border line. The task was not an easy one.

There is never a cause so weak that it does not stir into ill-timed activity some wild, unpractical zealots who imagine it strong. There is never a cause so just but that the malevolent and the mercenary will seek to trade upon it. The South was helpless; the one thing needful was to get it on its feet, and though the bravest and the wisest saw this plainly enough there came to the front—particularly in Kentucky—a small but noisy body of politicians who had only worked themselves into a state of war when it was too late, and who with more or less of aggression, insisted that "the states lately in rebellion" still had rights, which they were able to maintain and which the North could be forced to respect.

I was of a different opinion. It seemed to me that whatever of right might exist the South was at the mercy of the North; that the radical party led by Stevens and Wade dominated the North and could dictate its own terms; and that the shortest way round lay in that course which was best calculated to disarm radicalism by an intelligent appeal to the business interests and conservative elements of Northern society, supported by a domestic policy of justice alike to whites and blacks.

Though the institution of African slavery was gone the negro continued the subject of savage contention. I urged that he be taken out of the arena of agitation, and my way of taking him out was to concede him his legal and civil rights. The lately ratified Constitutional Amendments, I contended, were the real Treaty of Peace between the North and South. The recognition of these Amendments in good faith by the white people of the South was indispensable to that perfect peace which was desired by the best people of both sections. The political emancipation of the blacks was essential to the moral emancipation of the whites. With the disappearance of the negro question as cause of agitation, I argued, radicalism of the intense, proscriptive sort would die out; the liberty-loving, patriotic people of the North would assert themselves; and, this one obstacle to a better understanding removed, the restoration of Constitutional Government would follow, being a matter of momentous concern to the body of the people both North and South.

Such a policy of conciliation suited the Southern extremists as little as it suited the Northern extremists. It took from the politicians their best card. South no less than North, "the bloody shirt" was trumps. It could always be played. It was easy to play it and it never failed to catch the unthinking and to arouse the excitable. What cared the perennial candidate so he got votes enough? What cared the professional agitator so his appeals to passion brought him his audience?

It is a fact that until Lamar delivered his eulogy on Sumner not a Southern man of prominence used language calculated to placate the North, and between Lamar and Grady there was an interval of fifteen years. There was not a Democratic press worthy the name either North or South. During those evil days the Courier-Journal stood alone, having no party or organized following. At length it was joined on the Northern side by Greeley. Then Schurz raised his mighty voice. Then came the great liberal movement of 1871-72, with its brilliant but ill-starred campaign and its tragic finale; and then there set in what, for a season, seemed the deluge.

But the cause of Constitutional Government was not dead. It had been merely dormant. Champions began to appear in unexpected quarters. New men spoke up, North and South. In spite of the Republican landslide of 1872, in 1874 the Democrats swept the Empire State. They carried the popular branch of Congress by an overwhelming majority. In the Senate they had a respectable minority, with Thurman and Bayard to lead it. In the House Randall and Kerr and Cox, Lamar, Beck and Knott were about to be reënforced by Hill and Tucker and Mills and Gibson. The logic of events was at length subduing the rodomontade of soap-box oratory. Empty rant was to yield to reason. For all its mischances and melancholy ending the Greeley campaign had shortened the distance across the bloody chasm.

Chapter the Eighth

Feminism and Woman Suffrage — The Adventures in Politics and Society — A
Real Heroine

I

It would not be the writer of this narrative if he did not interject certain opinions of his own which parties and politicians, even his newspaper colleagues, have been wont to regard as peculiar. By common repute he has been an all-round old-line Democrat of the regulation sort. Yet on the three leading national questions of the last fifty years — the Negro question, the Greenback question and the Free Silver question — he has challenged and antagonized the general direction of that party. He takes some pride to himself that in each instance the result vindicated alike his forecast and his insubordination.

To one who witnessed the break-up of the Whig party in 1853 and of the Democratic Party in 1860 the plight in which parties find themselves at this time may be described as at least, suggestive. The feeling is at once to laugh and to whistle. Too much "fuss and feathers" in Winfield Scott did the business for the Whigs. Too much "bearded lady" in Charles Evans Hughes perhaps cooked the goose of the Republicans. Too much Wilson — but let me not fall into *lèse majesté*. The Whigs went into Know-Nothingism and Free Soilism. Will the Democrats go into Prohibition and paternalism? And the Republicans —

The old sectional alignment of North and South has been changed to East and

West.

For the time being the politicians of both parties are in something of a funk. It is the nature of parties thus situate to fancy that there is no hereafter, riding in their dire confusion headlong for a fall. Little other than the labels being left, nobody can tell what will happen to either.

Progressivism seems the cant of the indifferent. Accentuated by the indecisive vote in the elections and heralded by an ambitious President who writes Humanity bigger than he writes the United States, and is accused of aspiring to world leadership, democracy unterrified and undefiled—the democracy of Jefferson, Jackson and Tilden ancient history—has become a back number. Yet our officials still swear to a Constitution. We have not eliminated state lines. State rights are not wholly dead.

The fight between capital and labor is on. No one can predict where it will end. Shall it prove another irrepressible conflict? Are its issues irreconcilable? Must the alternative of the future lie between Socialism and Civil War, or both? Progress! Progress! Shall there be no stability in either actualities or principles? And—and— what about the Bolsheviki?

II

Parties, like men, have their ups and downs. Like machines they get out of whack and line. First it was the Federalists, then the Whigs, and then the Democrats. Then came the Republicans. And then, after a long interruption, the Democrats again. English political experience repeats itself in America.

A taking label is as valuable to a party as it is to a nostrum. It becomes in time an asset. We are told that a fool is born every minute, and, the average man being something of a fool, the label easily catches him. Hence the Democratic Party and the Republican Party.

The old Whig Party went to pieces on the rocks of sectionalism. The institution of African slavery arrived upon the scene at length as the paramount political issue. The North, which brought the Africans here in its ships, finding slave labor unprofitable, sold its slaves to the South at a good price, and turned pious. The South took the bait and went crazy.

Finally, we had a pretty kettle of fish. Just as the Prohibitionists are going to convert mortals into angels overnight by act of assembly—or still better, by Constitutional amendment—were the short-haired women and the long-haired men of Boston going to make a white man out of the black man by Abolition. The Southern Whigs could not see it and would not stand for it. So they fell in behind the Democrats. The Northern Whigs, having nowhere else to go, joined the Republicans.

The wise men of both sections saw danger ahead. The North was warned that the South would fight, the South, that if it did it went against incredible odds. Neither would take the warning. Party spirit ran wild. Extremism had its fling. Thus a long, bloody and costly War of Sections—a fraternal war if ever there was one— brought on by alternating intolerance, the politicians of both sides gambling upon the credulity and ignorance of the people.

Hindsight is readier, certainly surer, than foresight. It comes easier and shows clearer. Anybody can now see that the slavery problem might have had a less ruinous solution; that the moral issue might have been compromised from time to time and in the end disposed of. Slave labor even at the South had shown itself illusory, costly and clumsy. The institution untenable, modern thought against it, from the first it was doomed.

But the extremists would not have it. Each played to the lead of the other. Whilst Wendell Phillips was preaching the equality of races, death to the slaveholders and the brotherhood of man at the North, William Lowndes Yancey was exclaiming that cotton was king at the South, and, to establish these false propositions, millions of good Americans proceeded to cut one another's throats.

There were agitators and agitators in those days as there are in these. The agitator, like the poor, we have always with us. It used to be said even at the North that Wendell Phillips was just a clever comedian. William Lowndes Yancey was scarcely that. He was a serious, sincere, untraveled provincial, possessing unusual gifts of oratory. He had the misfortune to kill a friend in a duel when a young man, and the tragedy shadowed his life. He clung to his plantation and rarely went away from home. When sent to Europe by the South as its Ambassador in 1861, he discovered the futility of his scheme of a Southern confederacy, and, seeing the cornerstone of the philosophy on which he had constructed his pretty fabric, overthrown, he came home despairing, to die of a broken heart.

The moral alike for governments and men is: Keep the middle of the road.

III

Which brings us to Feminism. I will not write Woman Suffrage, for that is an accomplished fact—for good or evil we shall presently be better able to determine.

Life is an adventure and all of us adventurers—saving that the word presses somewhat harder upon the woman than the man—most things do in fact, whereby she is given greater endurance—leaving to men the duty of caring for the women; and, if need be, looking death squarely and defiantly in the face.

The world often puts the artificial before the actual; but under the dispensation of the Christian civilization—derived from the Hebraic—the family requiring a head, headship is assigned to the male. This male is commonly not much to speak of for beauty of form or decency of behavior. He is made purposely tough for work and fight. He gets toughened by outer contact. But back of all are the women, the children and the home.

I have been fighting the woman's battle for equality in the things that count, all my life. I would despise myself if I had not been. In contesting precipitate universal suffrage for women, I conceived that I was still fighting the woman's battle.

116

We can escape none of Nature's laws. But we need not handicap ourselves with artificial laws. At best, life is an experiment, Death the final adventure. Feminism seems to me its next of kin; still we may not call the woman who assails the soap boxes—even those that antic about the White House gates—by the opprobrious terms of adventuress. Where such a one is not a lunatic she is a nuisance. There are women and women.

We may leave out of account the shady ladies of history. Neither Aspasia nor Lucrezia Borgia nor the Marquise de Brinvilliers could with accuracy be called an adventuress. The term is of later date. Its origin and growth have arisen out of the complexities of modern society.

In fiction Milady and Madame Marneffe come in for first honors—in each the leopard crossed on the serpent and united under a petticoat, beautiful and wicked—but since the Balzac and Dumas days the story-tellers and stage-mongers have made exceeding free with the type, and we have between Herman Merivale's Stephanie de Mohrivart and Victorien Sardou's Zica a very theater—or shall we say a charnel house—of the woman with the past; usually portrayed as the victim of circumstance; unprincipled through cruel experience; insensible through lack of conscience; sexless in soul, but a siren in seductive arts; cold as ice; hard as iron; implacable as the grave, pursuing her ends with force of will, intellectual audacity and elegance of manner, yet, beneath this brilliant depravity, capable of self-pity, yielding anon in moments of depression to a sudden gleam of human tenderness and a certain regret for the innocence she has lost.

Such a one is sometimes, though seldom, met in real life. But many pretenders may be encountered at Monte Carlo and other European resorts. They range from the Parisian cocotte, signalized by her chic apparel, to the fashionable divorcée who in trying her luck at the tables keeps a sharp lookout for the elderly gent with the wad, often fooled by the enterprising sport who has been there before.

These are out and out professional adventuresses. There are other adventuresses, however, than those of the story and the stage, the casino and the cabaret. The woman with the past becomes the girl with the future.

Curiously enough this latter is mainly, almost exclusively, recruited from our countrywomen, who to an abnormal passion for foreign titles join surpassing ignorance of foreign society. Thus she is ready to the hand of the Continental fortune seeker masquerading as a nobleman — occasionally but not often the black sheep of some noble family — carrying not a bona fide but a courtesy title — the count and the no-account, the lord and the Lord knows who! The Yankee girl with a *dot* had become before the world war a regular quarry for impecunious aristocrats and clever crooks, the matrimonial results tragic in their frequency and squalor.

Another curious circumstance is the readiness with which the American newspaper tumbles to these frauds. The yellow press especially luxuriates in them; woodcuts the callow bedizened bride, the jaded game-worn groom; dilates upon the big money interchanged; glows over the tin-plate stars and imaginary garters and pinchbeck crowns; and keeping the pictorial paraphernalia in cold but not forgotten storage waits for the inevitable scandal, and then, with lavish exaggeration, works the old story over again.

These newspapers ring all the sensational changes. Now it is the wondrous beauty with the cool million, who, having married some illegitimate of a minor royal house, will probably be the next Queen of Rigmarolia, and now — ever increasing the dose — it is the ten-million-dollar widow who is going to marry the King of Pontarabia's brother, and may thus aspire to be one day Empress of Sahara.

Old European travelers can recall many funny and sometimes melancholy incidents — episodes — histories — of which they have witnessed the beginning and the end, carrying the self-same dénouement and lesson.

IV

As there are women and women there are many kinds of adventuresses; not all of them wicked and detestable. But, good or bad, the lot of the adventuress is at best a hard lot. Be she a girl with a future or a woman with a past she is still a woman, and the world can never be too kind to its women—the child bearers, the home makers, the moral light of the universe as they meet the purpose of God and Nature and seek not to thwart it by unsexing themselves in order that they may keep step with man in ways of self-indulgent dalliance. The adventuress of fiction always comes to grief. But the adventuress in real life—the prudent adventuress who draws the line at adultery—the would-be leader of society without the wealth—the would-be political leader without the masculine fiber—is sure of disappointment in the end.

Take the agitation over Suffragism. What is it that the woman suffragette expects to get? No one of them can, or does, clearly tell us.

It is feminism, rather than suffragism, which is dangerous. Now that they have it, my fear is that the leaders will not stop with the ballot for women. They are too fond of the spotlight. It has become a necessity for them. If all women should fall in with them there would be nothing of womanhood left, and the world bereft of its women will become a masculine harlotocracy.

Let me repeat that I have been fighting woman's battles in one way and another all my life. I am not opposed to Votes for Women. But I would discriminate and educate, and even at that rate I would limit the franchise to actual taxpayers, and, outside of these, confine it to charities, corrections and schools, keeping woman away from the dirt of politics. I do not believe the ballot will benefit woman and cannot help thinking that in seeking unlimited and precipitate suffrage the women who favor it are off their reckoning! I doubt the performances got up to exploit it, though somehow, when the hikers started from New York to Albany, and afterward from New York to Washington, the inspiring thought of Bertha von Hillern came back to me.

I am sure the reader never heard of her. As it makes a pretty story let me tell it. Many years ago—don't ask me how many—there was a young woman, Bertha von Hillern by name, a poor art student seeking money enough to take her abroad, who engaged with the management of a hall in Louisville to walk one hundred miles around a fixed track in twenty-four consecutive hours. She did it. Her share of the gate money, I was told, amounted to three thousand dollars.

I shall never forget the closing scenes of the wondrous test of courage and endurance. She was a pretty, fair-haired thing, a trifle undersized, but shapely and sinewy. The vast crowd that without much diminution, though with intermittent changes, had watched her from start to finish, began to grow tense with the approach to the end, and the last hour the enthusiasm was overwhelming. Wave upon wave of cheering followed every footstep of the plucky girl, rising to a storm of exultation as the final lap was reached.

More dead than alive, but game to the core, the little heroine was carried off the field, a winner, every heart throbbing with human sympathy, every eye wet with proud and happy tears. It is not possible adequately to describe all that happened. One must have been there and seen it fully to comprehend the glory of it.

Touching the recent Albany and Washington hikes and hikers let me say at once that I cannot approve the cause of Votes for women as I had approved the cause of Bertha von Hillern. Where she showed heroic, most of the suffragettes appear to me grotesque. Where her aim was rational, their aim has been visionary. To me the younger of them seem as children who need to be spanked and kissed. There has been indeed about the whole Suffrage business something pitiful and comic.

Often I have felt like swearing "You idiots!" and then like crying "Poor dears!" But I have kept on with them, and had I been in Albany or Washington I would have caught Rosalie Jones in my arms, and before she could say "Jack Robinson" have exclaimed: "You ridiculous child, go and get a bath and put on some pretty clothes and come and join us at dinner in the State Banquet Hall, duly made and provided for you and the rest of you delightful sillies."

Chapter the Ninth

Dr. Norvin Green—Joseph Pulitzer—Chester A. Arthur—General Grant—The Case of Fitz-John Porter

I

Truth we are told is stranger than fiction. I have found it so in the knowledge which has variously come to me of many interesting men and women. Of these Dr. Norvin Green was a striking example. To have sprung from humble parentage in the wilds of Kentucky and to die at the head of the most potential corporation in the world—to have held this place against all comers by force of abilities deemed indispensable to its welfare—to have gone the while his ain gait, disdaining the precepts of Doctor Franklin—who, by the way, did not trouble overmuch to follow them himself—seems so unusual as to rival the most stirring stories of the novel mongers.

When I first met Doctor Green he was president of a Kentucky railway company. He had been, however, one of the organizers of the Western Union Telegraph Company. He deluded himself for a little by political ambitions. He wanted to go to the Senate of the United States, and during a legislative session of prolonged balloting at Frankfort he missed his election by a single vote.

It may be doubted whether he would have cut a considerable figure at Washington. His talents were constructive rather than declamatory. He was called to a greater field—though he never thought it so—and was foremost among those who developed the telegraph system of the country almost from its infancy. He possessed the daring of the typical Kentuckian, with the dead calm of the stoic philosopher; imperturbable; never vexed or querulous or excited;

denying himself none of the indulgences of the gentleman of leisure. We grew to be constant comrades and friends, and when he returned to New York to take the important post which to the end of his days he filled so completely his office in the Western Union Building became my downtown headquarters.

There I met Jay Gould familiarly; and resumed acquaintance with Russell Sage, whom I had known when a lad in Washington, he a hayseed member of Congress; and occasionally other of the Wall Street leaders. In a small way—though not for long—I caught the stock-gambling fever. But I was on the "inside," and it was a cold day when I did not "clean up" a goodly amount to waste uptown in the evening. I may say that I gave this over through sheer disgust of acquiring so much and such easy and useless money, for, having no natural love of money—no aptitude for making money breed—no taste for getting it except to spend it—earning by my own accustomed and fruitful toil always a sufficiency—the distractions and dissipations it brought to my annual vacations and occasional visits, affronted in a way my self-respect, and palled upon my rather eager quest of pleasure. Money is purely relative. The root of all evil, too. Too much of it may bring ills as great as not enough.

At the outset of my stock-gambling experience I was one day in the office of President Edward H. Green, of the Louisville and Nashville Railway, no relation of Dr. Norvin Green, but the husband of the famous Hetty Green. He said to me, "How are you in stocks?"

"What do you mean?" said I.

"Why," he said, "do you buy long, or short? Are you lucky or unlucky?"

"You are talking Greek to me," I answered.

"Didn't you ever put up any money on a margin?"

"Never."

"Bless me! You are a virgin. I want to try your luck. Look over this stock list and pick a stock. I will take a crack at it. All I make we'll divide, and all we lose I'll pay."

"Will you leave this open for an hour or two?"

"What is the matter with it—is it not liberal enough?"

"The matter is that I am going over to the Western Union to lunch. The Gould party is to sit in with the Orton-Green party for the first time after their fight, and I am asked especially to be there. I may pick up something."

Big Green, as he was called, paused a moment reflectively. "I don't want any tip—especially from that bunch," said he. "I want to try your virgin luck. But, go ahead, and let me know this afternoon."

At luncheon I sat at Doctor Green's right, Jay Gould at his left. For the first and last time in its history wine was served at this board; Russell Sage was effusive in his demonstrations of affection and went on with his stories of my boyhood; every one sought to take the chill off the occasion; and we had a most enjoyable time instead of what promised to be rather a frosty formality. When the rest had departed, leaving Doctor Green, Mr. Gould and myself at table, mindful of what I had come for, in a bantering way I said to Doctor Green: "Now that I am a Wall Street ingénu, why don't you tell me something?"

Gould leaned across the table and said in his velvet voice: "Buy
Texas
Pacific."

Two or three days after, Texas Pacific fell off sixty points or more. I did not see Big Green again. Five or six months later I received from him a statement of account which I could never have unraveled, with a check for some thousands of dollars, my one-half profit on such and such an operation. Texas Pacific had come back again.

Two or three years later I sat at Doctor Green's table with Mr. Gould, just as we had sat the first day. Mr. Gould recalled the circumstance.

"I did not think I could afford to have you lose on my suggestion and I went to cover your loss, when I found five thousand shares of Texas Pacific transferred on the books of the company in your name. I knew these could not be yours. I thought the buyer was none other than the man I was after, and I began hammering the stock. I have been curious ever since to make sure whether I was right."

"Whom did you suspect, Mr. Gould?" I asked.

"My suspect was Victor Newcomb," he replied.

I then told him what had happened. "Dear, dear," he cried. "Ned Green! Big Green. Well, well! You do surprise me. I would rather have done him a favor than an injury. I am rejoiced to learn that no harm was done and that, after all, you and he came out ahead."

It was about this time Jay Gould had bought of the Thomas A. Scott estate a New York daily newspaper which, in spite of brilliant writers like Manton Marble and William Henry Hurlbut, had never been a moneymaker. This was the *World*. He offered me the editorship with forty-nine of the hundred shares of stock on very easy terms, which nowise tempted me. But two or three years after, I daresay both weary and hopeless of putting up so much money on an unyielding investment, he was willing to sell outright, and Joseph Pulitzer became the purchaser.

His career is another illustration of the saying that truth is stranger than fiction.

II

Joseph Pulitzer and I came together familiarly at the Liberal Republican Convention, which met at Cincinnati in 1872 — the convocation of cranks, as it was called — and nominated Horace Greeley for President. He was a delegate from Missouri. Subsequent events threw us much together. He began his English newspaper experience after a kind of apprenticeship on a German daily with Stilson Hutchins, another interesting character of those days. It was from Stilson Hutchins that I learned something of Pulitzer's origin and beginnings, for he never spoke much of himself.

According to this story he was the offspring of a runaway marriage between a subaltern officer in the Austrian service and a Hungarian lady of noble birth. In some way he had got across the Atlantic, and being in Boston, a wizened youth not speaking a word of English, he was spirited on board a warship. Watching his chance of escape he leaped overboard in the darkness of night, though it was the dead of winter, and swam ashore. He was found unconscious on the beach by some charitable persons, who cared for him. Thence he tramped it to St. Louis, where he heard there was a German colony, and found work on a coal barge.

It was here that the journalistic instinct dawned upon him. He began to carry river news items to the Westliche Post, which presently took him on its staff of regular reporters.

The rest was easy. He learned to speak and write English, was transferred to the paper of which Hutchins was the head, and before he was five-and-twenty became a local figure.

When he turned up in New York with an offer to purchase the World we met as old friends. During the interval between 1872 and 1883 we had had a runabout in Europe and I was able to render him assistance in the purchase proceeding he was having with Gould. When this was completed he said to me: "You are at entire leisure; you are worse than that, you are wasting your time about the clubs and watering places, doing no good for yourself, or anybody else. I must first devote myself to the reorganization of the business end of it. Here is a blank check. Fill it for whatever amount you please and it will be honored. I want you to go upstairs and organize my editorial force for me."

Indignantly I replied: "Go to the devil—you have not money enough—there is not money enough in the universe—to buy an hour of my season's loaf."

A year later I found him occupying with his family a splendid mansion up the Hudson, with a great stable of carriages and horses, living like a country gentleman, going to the World office about time for luncheon and coming away in the early afternoon. I passed a week-end with him. To me it seemed the precursor of ruin. His second payment was yet to be made. Had I been in his place I would have been taking my meals in an adjacent hotel, sleeping on a cot in one of the editorial rooms and working fifteen hours out of the twenty-four. To me it seemed dollars to doughnuts that he would break down and go to smash. But he did not—another case of destiny.

I was abiding with my family at Monte Carlo, when in his floating palace, the Liberty, he came into the harbor of Mentone. Then he bought a shore palace at Cap Martin. That season, and the next two or three seasons, we made voyages together from one end to the other of the Mediterranean, visiting the islands, especially Corsica and Elba, shrines of Napoleon whom he greatly admired.

He was a model host. He had surrounded himself with every luxury, including some agreeable retainers, and lived like a prince aboard. His blindness had already overtaken him. Other physical ailments assailed him. But no word of complaint escaped his lips and he rarely failed to sit at the head of his table. It was both splendid and pitiful.

Absolute authority made Pulitzer a tyrant. He regarded his newspaper ownership as an autocracy. There was nothing gentle in his domination, nor, I might say, generous either. He seriously lacked the sense of humor, and even among his familiars could never take a joke. His love of money was by no means inordinate. He spent it freely though not wastefully or joyously, for the possession of it rather flattered his vanity than made occasion for pleasure. Ability of varying kinds and degrees he had, a veritable genius for journalism and a real capacity for affection. He held his friends at good account and liked to have them about him. During the early days of his success he was disposed to overindulgence, not to say conviviality. He was fond of Rhine wines and an excellent judge of them, keeping a varied assortment always at hand. Once, upon the Liberty, he observed that I preferred a certain vintage. "You like this wine?" he said inquiringly. I assented, and he said, "I have a lot of it at home, and when I get back I will send you some." I had quite forgotten when, many months after, there came to me a crate containing enough to last me a life-time.

He had a retentive memory and rarely forgot anything. I could recall many pleasurable incidents of our prolonged and varied intimacy. We were one day wandering about the Montmartre region of Paris when we came into a hole-in-the-wall where they were playing a piece called "Les Brigands." It was melodrama to the very marrow of the bones of the Apaches that gathered and glared about. In those days, the "indemnity" paid and the "military occupation" withdrawn, everything French pre-figured hatred of the German, and be sure "Les Brigands" made the most of this; each "brigand" a beer-guzzling Teuton; each hero a dare-devil Gaul; and, when Joan the Maid, heroine, sent Goetz von Berlichingen, the Vandal Chieftain, sprawling in the saw-dust, there was no end to the enthusiasm.

"We are all 'brigands'," said Pulitzer as we came away, "differing according to individual character, to race and pursuit. Now, if I were writing that play, I should represent the villain as a tyrannous City Editor, meanly executing the orders of a niggardly proprietor."

"And the heroine?" I said.

"She should be a beautiful and rich young lady," he replied, "who buys the newspaper and marries the cub—rescuing genius from poverty and persecution."

He was not then the owner of the World. He had not created the Post-Dispatch, or even met the beautiful woman who became his wife. He was a youngster of five or six and twenty, revisiting the scenes of his boyhood on the beautiful blue Danube, and taking in Paris for a lark.

III

I first met General Grant in my own house. I had often been invited to his house. As far back as 1870 John Russell Young, a friend from boyhood, came with an invitation to pass the week-end as the President's guest at Long Branch. Many of my friends had cottages there. Of afternoons and evenings they played an infinitesimal game of draw poker.

"John," my answer was, "I don't dare to do so. I know that I shall fall in love with General Grant. We are living in rough times—particularly in rough party times. We have a rough presidential campaign ahead of us. If I go down to the seashore and go in swimming and play penny-ante with General Grant I shall not be able to do my duty."

It was thus that after the general had gone out of office and made the famous journey round the world, and had come to visit relatives in Kentucky, that he accepted a dinner invitation from me, and I had a number of his friends to meet him.

Among these were Dr. Richardson, his early schoolmaster when the Grant family lived at Maysville, and Walter Haldeman, my business partner, a Maysville boy, who had been his schoolmate at the Richardson Academy, and General Cerro Gordo Williams, then one of Kentucky's Senators in Congress, and erst his comrade and chum when both were lieutenants in the Mexican War. The bars were down, the windows were shut and there was no end of hearty hilarity. Dr. Richardson had been mentioned by Mr. Haldeman as "the only man that ever licked Grant," and the general promptly retorted "he never licked me," when the good old doctor said, "No, Ulysses, I never did—nor Walter, either—for you two were the best boys in school."

I said "General Grant, why not give up this beastly politics, buy a blue-grass farm, and settle down to horse-raising and tobacco growing in Kentucky?" And, quick as a flash—for both he and the company perceived that it was "a leading question"—he replied, "Before I can buy a farm in Kentucky I shall have to sell a farm in Missouri," which left nothing further to be said.

There was some sparring between him and General Williams over their youthful adventures. Finally General Williams, one of the readiest and most amusing of talkers, returned one of General Grant's sallies with, "Anyhow, I know of a man whose life you took unknown to yourself." Then he told of a race he and Grant had outside of Galapa in 1846. "Don't you remember," he said, "that riding ahead of me you came upon a Mexican loaded with a lot of milk cans piled above his head and that you knocked him over as you swept by him?"

"Yes," said Grant, "I believed if I stopped or questioned or even deflected it would lose me the race. I have not thought of it since. But now that you mention it I recall it distinctly."

128

"Well," Williams continued, "you killed him. Your horse's hoof struck him. When, seeing I was beaten, I rode back, his head was split wide open. I did not tell you at the time because I knew it would cause you pain, and a dead greaser more or less made no difference."

Later on General Grant took desk room in Victor Newcomb's private office in New York. There I saw much of him, and we became good friends. He was the most interesting of men. Soldierlike—monosyllabic—in his official and business dealings he threw aside all formality and reserve in his social intercourse, delightfully reminiscential, indeed a capital story teller. I do not wonder that he had constant and disinterested friends who loved him sincerely.

IV

It has always been my opinion that if Chester A. Arthur had been named by the Republicans as their candidate in 1884 they would have carried the election, spite of what Mr. Blaine, who defeated Arthur in the convention, had said and thought about the nomination of General Sherman. Arthur, like Grant, belonged to the category of lovable men in public life.

There was a gallant captain in the army who had slapped his colonel in the face on parade. Morally, as man to man, he had the right of it. But military law is inexorable. The verdict was dismissal from the service. I went with the poor fellow's wife and her sister to see General Hancock at Governor's Island. It was a most affecting meeting—the general, tears rolling down his cheeks, taking them into his arms, and, when he could speak, saying: "I can do nothing but hold up the action of the court till Monday. Your recourse is the President and a pardon; I will recommend it, but"—putting his hand upon my shoulder—"here is the man to get the pardon if the President can be brought to see the case as most of us see it."

At once I went over to Washington, taking Stephen French with me. When we entered the President's apartment in the White House he advanced smiling to greet us, saying: "I know what you boys are after; you mean—"

"Yes, Mr. President," I answered, "we do, and if ever—"

"I have thought over it, sworn over it, and prayed over it," he said, "and
I am going to pardon him!"

V

Another illustrative incident happened during the Arthur Administration. The dismissal of Gen. Fitz-John Porter from the army had been the subject of more or less acrimonious controversy. During nearly two decades this had raged in army circles. At length the friends of Porter, led by Curtin and Slocum, succeeded in passing a relief measure through Congress. They were in ecstasies. That there might be a presidential objection had not crossed their minds.

Senator McDonald, of Indiana, a near friend of General Porter, and a man of rare worldly wisdom, knew better. Without consulting them he came to me.

"You are personally close to the President," said he, "and you must know that if this bill gets to the White House he will veto it. With the Republican National Convention directly ahead he is bound to veto it. It must not be allowed to get to him; and you are the man to stop it. They will listen to you and will not listen to me."

First of all, I went to the White House.

"Mr. President," I said, "I want you to authorize me to tell Curtin and
Slocum not to send the Fitz-John Porter bill to you."

"Why?" he answered.

"Because," said I, "you will have to veto it; and, with the Frelinghuysens wild for it, as well as others of your nearest friends, I am sure you don't want to be obliged to do that. With your word to me I can stop it, and have it for the present at least held up."

His answer was, "Go ahead."

Then I went to the Capitol. Curtin and Slocum were in a state of mind. It was hard to make them understand or believe what I told them.

"Now, gentlemen," I continued, "I don't mean to argue the case. It is not debatable. I am just from the White House, and I am authorized by the President to say that if you send this bill to him he will veto it."

That, of course, settled it. They held it up. But after the presidential election it reached Arthur, and he did veto it. Not till Cleveland came in did Porter obtain his restoration.

Curiously enough General Grant approved this. I had listened to the debate in the House — especially the masterly speech of William Walter Phelps — without attaining a clear understanding of the many points at issue. I said as much to General Grant.

"Why," he replied, "the case is as simple as A, B, C. Let me show you."

Then, with a pencil he traced the Second Bull Run battlefield, the location of troops, both Federal and Confederate, and the exact passage in the action which had compromised General Porter.

"If Porter had done what he was ordered to do," he went on, "Pope and his army would have been annihilated. In point of fact Porter saved Pope's Army." Then he paused and added: "I did not at the outset know this. I was for a time of a different opinion and on the other side. It was Longstreet's testimony — which had not been before the first Court of Inquiry that convicted Porter — which vindicated him and convinced me."

Chapter the Tenth

Of Liars and Lying — Woman Suffrage and Feminism — The Professional
Female — Parties, Politics, and Politicians in America

I

All is fair in love and war, the saying hath it. "Lord!" cried the most delightful of liars, "How this world is given to lying." Yea, and how exigency quickens invention and promotes deceit.

Just after the war of sections I was riding in a train with Samuel Bowles, who took a great interest in things Southern. He had been impressed by a newspaper known as The Chattanooga Rebel and, as I had been its editor, put innumerable questions to me about it and its affairs. Among these he asked how great had been its circulation. Without explaining that often an entire company, in some cases an entire regiment, subscribed for a few copies, or a single copy, I answered: "I don't know precisely, but somewhere near a hundred thousand, I take it." Then he said: "Where did you get your press power?"

This was, of course, a poser, but it did not embarrass me in the least. I was committed, and without a moment's thought I proceeded with an imaginary explanation which he afterward declared had been altogether satisfying. The story was too good to keep — maybe conscience pricked — and in a chummy talk later along I laughingly confessed.

"You should tell that in your dinner speech tonight," he said. "If you tell it as you have just told it to me, it will make a hit," and I did.

I give it as the opinion of a long life of experience and observation that the newspaper press, whatever its delinquencies, is not a common liar, but the most habitual of truth tellers. It is growing on its editorial page I fear a little vapid and colorless. But there is a general and ever-present purpose to print the facts and give the public the opportunity to reach its own conclusions.

There are liars and liars, lying and lying. It is, with a single exception, the most universal and venial of human frailties. We have at least three kinds of lying and species, or types, of liars—first, the common, ordinary, everyday liar, who lies without rime or reason, rule or compass, aim, intent or interest, in whose mind the partition between truth and falsehood has fallen down; then the sensational, imaginative liar, who has a tale to tell; and, finally, the mean, malicious liar, who would injure his neighbor.

This last is, indeed, but rare. Human nature is at its base amicable, because if nothing hinders it wants to please. All of us, however, are more or less its unconscious victims.

Competition is not alone the life of trade; it is the life of life; for each of us is in one way, or another, competitive. There is but one disinterested person in the world, the mother who whether of the human or animal kingdom, will die for her young. Yet, after all, hers, too, is a kind of selfishness.

The woman is becoming over much a professional female. It is of importance that we begin to consider her as a new species, having enjoyed her beauty long enough. Is the world on the way to organic revolution? If I were a young man I should not care to be the lover of a professional female. As an old man I have affectionate relations with a number of suffragettes, as they dare not deny; that is to say, I long ago accepted woman suffrage as inevitable, whether for good or evil, depending upon whether the woman's movement is going to stop with suffrage or run into feminism, changing the character of woman and her relations to men and with man.

II

I have never made party differences the occasion of personal quarrel or estrangement. On the contrary, though I have been always called a Democrat, I have many near and dear friends among the Republicans. Politics is not war. Politics would not be war even if the politicians were consistent and honest. But there are among them so many changelings, cheats and rogues.

Then, in politics as elsewhere, circumstances alter cases. I have as a rule thought very little of parties as parties, professional politicians and party leaders, and I think less of them as I grow older. The politician and the auctioneer might be described like the lunatic, the lover and the poet, as "of imagination all compact." One sees more mares' nests than would fill a book; the other pure gold in pinchbeck wares; and both are out for gudgeons.

It is the habit—nay, the business—of the party speaker when he mounts the raging stump to roar his platitudes into the ears of those who have the simplicity to listen, though neither edified nor enlightened; to aver that the horse he rides is sixteen feet high; that the candidate he supports is a giant; and that he himself is no small figure of a man.

Thus he resembles the auctioneer. But it is the mock auctioneer whom he resembles; his stock in trade being largely, if not altogether, fraudulent. The success which at the outset of party welfare attended this legalized confidence game drew into it more and more players. For a long time they deceived themselves almost as much as the voters. They had not become professional. They were amateur. Many of them played for sheer love of the gamble. There were rules to regulate the play. But as time passed and voters multiplied, the popular preoccupation increased the temptations and opportunities for gain, inviting the enterprising, the skillful and the corrupt to reconstitute patriotism into a commodity and to organize public opinion into a bill of lading. Thus politics as a trade, parties as trademarks, the politicians, like harlots, plying their vocation.

Now and again an able, honest and brave man, who aims at better things, appears. In the event that fortune favors him and he attains high station, he finds himself surrounded and thwarted by men less able and courageous, who, however equal to discovering right from wrong, yet wear the party collar, owe fealty to the party machine, are sometimes actual slaves of the party boss. In the larger towns we hear of the City Hall ring; out in the counties of the Court House ring. We rarely anywhere encounter clean, responsible administration and pure, disinterested, public service.

The taxpayers are robbed before their eyes. The evil grows greater as we near the centers of population. But there is scarcely a village or hamlet where graft does not grow like weeds, the voters as gullible and helpless as the infatuated victims of bunko tricks, ingeniously contrived by professional crooks to separate the fool and his money. Is self-government a failure?

None of us would allow the votaries of the divine right of kings to tell us so, albeit we are ready enough to admit the imperfections of universal suffrage, too often committing affairs of pith and moment, even of life and death, to the arbitrament of the mob, and costing more in cash outlay than royal establishments.

The quadrennial period in American politics, set apart and dedicated to the election of presidents, magnifies these evil features in an otherwise admirable system of government. That the whipper-snappers of the vicinage should indulge their propensities comes as the order of their nature. But the party leaders are not far behind them. Each side construes every occurrence as an argument in its favor, assuring it certain victory. Take, for example, the latest state election anywhere. In point of fact, it foretold nothing. It threw no light upon coming events, not even upon current events. It leaves the future as hazy as before. Yet the managers of either party affect to be equally confident that it presages the triumph of their ticket in the next national election. The wonder is that so many of the voters will believe and be influenced by such transparent subterfuge.

Is there any remedy for all this? I much fear that there is not. Government, like all else, is impossible of perfection. It is as man is—good, bad and indifferent; which is but another way of saying we live in a world of cross purposes. We in America prefer republicanism. But would despotism be so demurrable under a wise unselfish despot?

III

Contemplating the contrasts between foreign life and foreign history with our own one cannot help reflecting upon the yet more startling contrasts of ancient and modern religion and government. I have wandered not a little over Europe at irregular intervals for more than fifty years. Always a devotee to American institutions, I have been strengthened in my beliefs by what I have encountered.

The mood in our countrymen has been overmuch to belittle things American. The commercial spirit in the United States, which affects to be nationalistic, is in reality cosmopolitan. Money being its god, French money, English money, anything that calls itself money, is wealth to it. It has no time to waste on theories or to think of generics. "Put money in thy purse" has become its motto. Money constitutes the reason of its being. The organic law of the land is Greek to it, as are those laws of God which obstruct it. It is too busy with its greed and gain to think, or to feel, on any abstract subject. That which does not appeal to it in the concrete is of no interest at all.

Just as in the days of Charles V and Philip II, all things yielded to the theologian's misconception of the spiritual life so in these days of the Billionaires all things spiritual and abstract yield to what they call the progress of the universe and the leading of the times. Under their rule we have had extraordinary movement just as under the lords of the Palatinate and the Escurial—the medieval union of the devils of bigotry and power—Europe, which was but another name for Spain, had extraordinary movement. We know where it ended with Spain. Whither is it leading us? Are we traveling the same road?

Let us hope not. Let us believe not. Yet, once strolling along through the crypt of the Church of the Escurial near Madrid, I could not repress the idea of a personal and physical resemblance between the effigies in marble and bronze looking down upon me whichever way I turned, to some of our contemporary public men and seeming to say: "My love to the President when you see him next," and

"Don't forget to remember me kindly, please, to the chairmen of both your national committees!"

IV

In a world of sin, disease and death — death inevitable — what may man do to drive out sin and cure disease, to the end that, barring accident, old age shall set the limit on mortal life?

The quack doctor equally in ethics and in physics has played a leading part in human affairs. Only within a relatively brief period has science made serious progress toward discovery. Though Nature has perhaps an antidote for all her posions many of them continue to defy approach. They lie concealed, leaving the astutest to grope in the dark.

That which is true of material things is truer yet of spiritual things. The ideal about which we hear so much, is as unattained as the fabled bag of gold at the end of the rainbow. Nor is the doctrine of perfectability anywhere one with itself. It speaks in diverse tongues. Its processes and objects are variant. It seems but an iridescent dream which lends itself equally to the fancies of the impracticable and the scheming of the self-seeking, breeding visionaries and pretenders.

Easily assumed and asserted, too often it becomes tyrannous, dealing with things outer and visible while taking little if any account of the inner lights of the soul. Thus it imposes upon credulity and ignorance; makes fakers of some and fanatics of others; in politics where not an engine of oppression, a corrupt influence; in religion where not a zealot, a promoter of cant. In short the self-appointed apostle of uplift, who disregarding individual character would make virtue a matter of statute law and ordain uniformity of conduct by act of conventicle or assembly, is likelier to produce moral chaos than to reach the sublime state he claims to seek.

The bare suggestion is full of startling possibilities. Individualism was the discovery of the fathers of the American Republic. It is the bedrock of our political philosophy. Human slavery was assuredly an indefensible institution. But the armed enforcement of freedom did not make a black man a white man. Nor will the wave of fanaticism seeking to control the food and drink and dress of the people make men better men. Danger lurks and is bound to come with the inevitable reaction.

The levity of the men is recruited by the folly of the women. The leaders of feminism would abolish sex. To what end? The pessimist answers what easier than the demolition of a sexless world gone entirely mad? How simple the engineries of destruction. Civil war in America; universal hara-kiri in Europe; the dry rot of wealth wasting itself in self-indulgence. Then a thousand years of total eclipse. Finally Macaulay's Australian surveying the ruins of St. Paul's Cathedral from a broken parapet of London Bridge; and a Moslem conqueror of America looking from the hill of the Capitol at Washington upon the desolation of what was once the District of Columbia. Shall the end be an Oriental renaissance with the philosophies of Buddha, Mohammed and Confucius welded into a new religion describing itself as the last word of science, reason and common sense?

Alas, and alack the day! In those places where the suffering rich most do congregate the words of Watts' hymn have constant application:

For Satan finds some mischief still
  For idle hands to do.

When they have not gone skylarking or grown tired of bridge they devote their leisure to organizing clubs other than those of the uplift. There are all sorts, from the Society for the Abrogation of Bathing Suits at the seaside resorts to the League at Mewville for the Care of Disabled Cats. Most of these clubs are all officers and no privates. That is what many of them are got up for. Do they advance the world in grace? One who surveys the scene can scarcely think so.

But the whirl goes on; the yachts sweep proudly out to sea; the auto cars dash madly through the streets; more and darker and deeper do the contrasts of life show themselves. How long shall it be when the mudsill millions take the upper ten thousand by the throat and rend them as the furiosos of the Terror in France did the aristocrats of the *Régime Ancien*? The issue between capital and labor, for example, is full of generating heat and hate. Who shall say that, let loose in the crowded centers of population, it may not one day engulf us all?

Is this rank pessimism or merely the vagaries of an old man dropping back into second childhood, who does not see that the world is wiser and better than ever it was, mankind and womankind, surely on the way to perfection?

V

One thing is certain: We are not standing still. Since "Adam delved and Eve span"—if they ever did—in the Garden of Eden, "somewhere in Asia," to the "goings on" in the Garden of the Gods directly under Pike's Peak—the earth we inhabit has at no time and nowhere wanted for liveliness—but surely it was never livelier than it now is; as the space-writer says, more "dramatic"; indeed, to quote the guidebooks, quite so "picturesque and interesting."

Go where one may, on land or sea, he will come upon activities of one sort and another. Were Timon of Athens living, he might be awakened from his misanthrophy and Jacques, the forest cynic, stirred to something like enthusiasm. Is the world enduring the pangs of a second birth which shall recreate all things anew, supplementing the miracles of modern invention with a corresponding development of spiritual life; or has it reached the top of the hill, and, mortal, like the human atoms that compose it, is it starting downward on the other side into an abyss which the historians of the future will once again call "the dark ages?"

We know not, and there is none to tell us. That which is actually happening were unbelievable if we did not see it, from hour to hour, from day to day. Horror succeeding horror has in some sort blunted our sensibilities. Not only are our sympathies numbed by the immensity of the slaughter and the sorrow, but patriotism itself is chilled by the selfish thought that, having thus far measurably escaped, we may pull through without paying our share. This will account for a certain indifferentism we now and again encounter.

At the moment we are felicitating ourselves — or, is it merely confusing ourselves? — over the revolution in Russia. It seems of good augury. To begin with, for Russia. Then the murder war fairly won for the Allies, we are promised by the optimists a wise and lasting peace.

The bells that rang out in Petrograd and Moscow sounded, we are told, the death knell of autocracy in Berlin and Vienna. The clarion tones that echoed through the Crimea and Siberia, albeit to the ear of the masses muffled in the Schwarzwald and along the shores of the North Sea, and up and down the Danube and the Rhine, yet conveyed a whispered message which may presently break into song; the glad song of freedom with it glorious refrain: "The Romanoffs gone! Perdition having reached the Hohenzollerns and the Hapsburgs, all will be well!"

Anyhow, freedom; self-government; for whilst a scrutinizing and solicitous pessimism, observing and considering many abuses, administrative and political, federal and local, in our republican system — abuses which being very visible are most lamentable — may sometimes move us to lose heart of hope in democracy, we know of none better. So, let us stand by it; pray for it; fight for it. Let us by our example show the Russians how to attain it. Let us by the same token show the Germans how to attain it when they come to see, if they ever do, the havoc autocracy has made for Germany. That should constitute the bed rock of our politics and our religion. It is the true religion. Love of country is love of God. Patriotism is religion.

It is also Christianity. The pacifist, let me parenthetically observe, is scarcely a Christian. There be technical Christians and there be Christians. The technical Christian sees nothing but the blurred letter of the law, which he misconstrues. The Christian, animated by its holy spirit and led by its rightful interpretation, serves the Lord alike of heaven and hosts when he flies the flag of his country and smites its enemies hip and thigh!

Chapter the Eleventh

Andrew Johnson — The Liberal Convention in 1872 — Carl Schurz — The
    "Quadrilateral" — Sam Bowles, Horace White and Murat Halstead — A Queer
    Composite of Incongruities

I

Among the many misconceptions and mischances that befell the slavery agitation in the United States and finally led a kindred people into actual war the idea that got afloat after this war that every Confederate was a Secessionist best served the ends of the radicalism which sought to reduce the South to a conquered province, and as such to reconstruct it by hostile legislation supported wherever needed by force.

Andrew Johnson very well understood that a great majority of the men who were arrayed on the Southern side had taken the field against their better judgment through pressure of circumstance. They were Union men who had opposed secession and clung to the old order. Not merely in the Border States did this class rule but in the Gulf States it held a respectable minority until the shot fired upon Sumter drew the call for troops from Lincoln. The Secession leaders, who had staked their all upon the hazard, knew that to save their movement from collapse it was necessary that blood be sprinkled in the faces of the people. Hence the message from Charleston:

With cannon, mortar and petard
  We tender you our Beauregard —

with the response from Washington precipitating the conflict of theories into a combat of arms for which neither party was prepared.

The debate ended, battle at hand, Southern men had to choose between the North and the South, between their convictions and predilections on one side and expatriation on the other side—resistance to invasion, not secession, the issue. But four years later, when in 1865 all that they had believed and feared in 1861 had come to pass, these men required no drastic measures to bring them to terms. Events more potent than acts of Congress had already reconstructed them. Lincoln with a forecast of this had shaped his ends accordingly. Johnson, himself a Southern man, understood it even better than Lincoln, and backed by the legacy of Lincoln he proceeded not very skillfully to build upon it.

The assassination of Lincoln, however, had played directly into the hands of the radicals, led by Ben Wade in the Senate and Thaddeus Stevens in the House. Prior to that baleful night they had fallen behind the marching van. The mad act of Booth put them upon their feet and brought them to the front. They were implacable men, politicians equally of resolution and ability. Events quickly succeeding favored them and their plans. It was not alone Johnson's lack of temper and tact that gave them the whip hand. His removal from office would have opened the door of the White House to Wade, so that strategically Johnson's position was from the beginning beleaguered and came perilously near before the close to being untenable.

Grant, a political nondescript, not Wade, the uncompromising extremist, came after; and inevitably four years of Grant had again divided the triumphant Republicans. This was the situation during the winter of 1871-72, when the approaching Presidential election brought the country face to face with a most extraordinary state of affairs. The South was in irons. The North was growing restive. Thinking people everywhere felt that conditions so anomalous to our institutions could not and should not endure.

II

Johnson had made a bungling attempt to carry out the policies of Lincoln and had gone down in the strife. The Democratic Party had reached the ebb tide of its disastrous fortunes.

It seemed the merest reactionary. A group of influential Republicans, dissatisfied for one cause and another with Grant, held a caucus and issued a call for what they described as a Liberal Republican Convention to assemble in Cincinnati May 1, 1872.

A Southern man and a Confederate soldier, a Democrat by conviction and inheritance, I had been making in Kentucky an uphill fight for the acceptance of the inevitable. The line of cleavage between the old and the new South I had placed upon the last three amendments to the Constitution, naming them the Treaty of Peace between the Sections. The negro must be invested with the rights conferred upon him by these amendments, however mistaken and injudicious the South might think them. The obsolete Black Laws instituted during the slave régime must be removed from the statute books. The negro, like Mohammed's coffin, swung in midair. He was neither fish, flesh nor fowl, nor good red herring. For our own sake we must habilitate him, educate and elevate him, make him, if possible, a contented and useful citizen. Failing of this, free government itself might be imperiled.

I had behind me the intelligence of the Confederate soldiers almost to a man. They at least were tired of futile fighting, and to them the war was over. But—and especially in Kentucky—there was an element that wanted to fight when it was too late; old Union Democrats and Union Whigs who clung to the hull of slavery when the kernel was gone, and proposed to win in politics what had been lost in battle.

The leaders of this belated element were in complete control of the political machinery of the state. They regarded me as an impudent upstart—since I had come to Kentucky from Tennessee—as little better than a carpet-bagger; and had done their uttermost to put me down and drive me out.

[Illustration: Abraham Lincoln in 1861 *From a Photograph by M B Brady*]

I was a young fellow of two and thirty, of boundless optimism and my full share of self-confidence, no end of physical endurance and mental vitality, having some political as well as newspaper experience. It never crossed my fancy that I could fail.

I met resistance with aggression, answered attempts at bullying with scorn, generally irradiated by laughter. Yet was I not wholly blind to consequences and the admonitions of prudence; and when the call for a Liberal Republican Convention appeared I realized that if I expected to remain a Democrat in a Democratic community, and to influence and lead a Democratic following, I must proceed warily.

Though many of those proposing the new movement were familiar acquaintances—some of them personal friends—the scheme was in the air, as it were. Its three newspaper bellwethers—Samuel Bowles, Horace White and Murat Halstead—were especially well known to me; so were Horace Greeley, Carl Schurz and Charles Sumner, Stanley Matthews being my kinsman, George Hoadley and Cassius M. Clay next-door neighbors. But they were not the men I had trained with—not my "crowd"—and it was a question how far I might be able to reconcile myself, not to mention my political associates, to such company, even conceding that they proceeded under good fortune with a good plan, offering the South extrication from its woes and the Democratic Party an entering wedge into a solid and hitherto irresistible North.

Nevertheless, I resolved to go a little in advance to Cincinnati, to have a look at the stalking horse there to be displayed, free to take it or leave it as I liked, my bridges and lines of communication quite open and intact.

III

A livelier and more variegated omnium-gatherum was never assembled. They had already begun to straggle in when I arrived. There were long-haired and spectacled doctrinaires from New England, spliced by short-haired and stumpy emissaries from New York—mostly friends of Horace Greeley, as it turned out. There were brisk Westerners from Chicago and St. Louis. If Whitelaw Reid, who had come as Greeley's personal representative, had his retinue, so had Horace White and Carl Schurz. There were a few rather overdressed persons from New Orleans brought up by Governor Warmouth, and a motely array of Southerners of every sort, who were ready to clutch at any straw that promised relief to intolerable conditions. The full contingent of Washington correspondents was there, of course, with sharpened eyes and pens to make the most of what they had already begun to christen a conclave of cranks.

Bowles and Halstead met me at the station, and we drove to the St. Nicholas Hotel, where Schurz and White were awaiting us. Then and there was organized a fellowship which in the succeeding campaign cut a considerable figure and went by the name of the Quadrilateral. We resolved to limit the Presidential nominations of the convention to Charles Francis Adams, Bowles' candidate, and Lyman Trumbull, White's candidate, omitting altogether, because of specific reasons urged by White, the candidacy of B. Gratz Brown, who because of his Kentucky connections had better suited my purpose.

The very next day the secret was abroad, and Whitelaw Reid came to me to ask why in a newspaper combine of this sort the New York Tribune had been left out.

To my mind it seemed preposterous that it had been or should be, and I stated as much to my new colleagues. They offered objection which to me appeared perverse if not childish. They did not like Reid, to begin with. He was not a principal like the rest of us, but a subordinate. Greeley was this, that and the other. He could never be relied upon in any coherent practical plan of campaign. To talk about him as a candidate was ridiculous.

I listened rather impatiently and finally I said: "Now, gentlemen, in this movement we shall need the New York Tribune. If we admit Reid we clinch it. You will all agree that Greeley has no chance of a nomination, and so by taking him in we both eat our cake and have it."

On this view of the case Reid was invited to join us, and that very night he sat with us at the St. Nicholas, where from night to night until the end we convened and went over the performances and developments of the day and concerted plans for the morrow.

As I recall these symposiums some amusing and some plaintive memories rise before me.

The first serious business that engaged us was the killing of the boom for Judge David Davis, of the Supreme Court, which was assuming definite and formidable proportions. The preceding winter it had been incubating at Washington under the ministration of some of the most astute politicians of the time, mainly, however, Democratic members of Congress.

A party of these had brought it to Cincinnati, opening headquarters well provided with the requisite commissaries. Every delegate who came in that could be reached was laid hold of and conducted to Davis' headquarters.

We considered it flat burglary. It was a gross infringement upon our copyrights. What business had the professional politicians with a great reform movement? The influence and dignity of journalism were at stake. The press was imperilled. We, its custodians, could brook no such deflection, not to say defiance, from intermeddling office seekers, especially from broken-down Democratic office seekers.

The inner sanctuary of our proceedings was a common drawing-room between two bedchambers, occupied by Schurz and myself. Here we repaired after supper to smoke the pipe of fraternity and reform, and to save the country. What might be done to kill off "D. Davis," as we irreverently called the eminent and learned jurist, the friend of Lincoln and the only aspirant having a "bar'l"? That was

the question. We addressed ourselves to the task with earnest purpose, but characteristically. The power of the press must be invo-
ked. It was our chief if not our only weapon. Seated at the same
table each of us indited a leading editorial for his paper, to be wired
to its destination and printed next morning, striking D. Davis at a
prearranged and varying angle. Copies of these were made for
Halstead, who having with the rest of us read and compared the
different scrolls indited one of his own in general commentation
and review for Cincinnati consumption. In next day's Commercial,
blazing under vivid headlines, these leading editorials, dated "Chicago" and "New York," "Springfield, Mass.," and "Louisville, Ky.,"
appeared with the explaining line "The Tribune of to-morrow morning will say—" "The Courier-Journal—and the Republican—will say
to-morrow morning—"

Wondrous consensus of public opinion! The Davis boom went
down before it. The Davis boomers were paralyzed. The earth seemed to have risen and hit them midships. The incoming delegates
were arrested and forewarned. Six months of adroit scheming was
set at naught, and little more was heard of "D. Davis."

We were, like the Mousquetaires, equally in for fighting and foot-
racing, the point with us being to get there, no matter how; the
end—the defeat of the rascally machine politicians and the reform
of the public service—justifying the means. I am writing this nearly
fifty years after the event and must be forgiven the fling of my wisdom at my own expense and that of my associates in harmless cri-
me.

Some ten years ago I wrote: "Reid and White and I the sole survi-
vors; Reid a great Ambassador, White and I the virtuous ones, still
able to sit up and take notice, with three meals a day for which we
are thankful and able to pay; no one of us recalcitrant. We were
wholly serious—maybe a trifle visionary, but as upright and patriotic in our intentions and as loyal to our engagements as it was possible for older and maybe better men to be. For my part I must say
that if I have never anything on my conscience worse than the mas-
sacre of that not very edifying yet promising combine I shall be
troubled by no remorse, but to the end shall sleep soundly and
well."

Alas, I am not the sole survivor. In this connection an amusing incident throwing some light upon the period thrusts itself upon my memory. The Quadrilateral, including Reid, had just finished its consolidation of public opinion before related, when the cards of Judge Craddock, chairman of the Kentucky Democratic Committee, and of Col. Stoddard Johnston, editor of the Frankfort Yeoman, the organ of the Kentucky Democracy, were brought from below. They had come to look after me—that was evident. By no chance could they find me in more equivocal company. In addition to ourselves—bad enough, from the Kentucky point of view—Theodore Tilton, Donn Piatt and David A. Wells were in the room.

When the Kentuckians crossed the threshold and were presented seriatim the face of each was a study. Even a proper and immediate application of whisky and water did not suffice to restore their lost equilibrium and bring them to their usual state of convivial self-possession. Colonel Johnston told me years after that when they went away they walked in silence a block or two, when the old judge, a model of the learned and sedate school of Kentucky politicians and jurists, turned to him and said: "It is no use, Stoddart, we cannot keep up with that young man or with these times. 'Lord, now lettest thou thy servant depart in peace!'"

IV

The Jupiter Tonans of reform in attendance upon the convention was Col. Alexander K. McClure. He was one of the handsomest and most imposing of men; Halstead himself scarcely more so. McClure was personally unknown to the Quadrilateral. But this did not stand in the way of our asking him to dine with us as soon as his claims to fellowship in the good cause of reform began to make themselves apparent through the need of bringing the Pennsylvania delegation to a realizing sense.

He looked like a god as he entered the room; nay, he acted like one. Schurz first took him in hand. With a lofty courtesy I have never seen equalled he tossed his inquisitor into the air. Halstead came next, and tried him upon another tack. He fared no better than Schurz. And hurrying to the rescue of my friends, McClure, looking now a bit bored and resentful, landed me somewhere near the ceiling.

It would have been laughable if it had not been ignominious. I took my discomfiture with the bad grace of silence throughout the stiff, formal and brief meal which was then announced. But when it was over and the party, risen from table, was about to disperse I collected my energies and resources for a final stroke. I was not willing to remain so crushed nor to confess myself so beaten, though I could not disguise from myself a feeling that all of us had been overmatched.

"McClure," said I with the cool and quiet resolution of despair, drawing him aside, "what in the — — do you want anyhow?"

He looked at me with swift intelligence and a sudden show of sympathy, and then over at the others with a withering glance.

"What? With those cranks? Nothing."

Jupiter descended to earth. I am afraid we actually took a glass of wine together. Anyhow, from that moment to the hour of his death we were the best of friends.

Without the inner circle of the Quadrilateral, which had taken matters into their own hands, were a number of persons, some of them disinterested and others simple curiosity and excitement seekers, who might be described as merely lookers-on in Vienna. The Sunday afternoon before the convention was to meet we, the self-elect, fell in with a party of these in a garden "over the Rhine," as the German quarter of Cincinnati is called. There was first general and rather aimless talk. Then came a great deal of speech making. Schurz started it with a few pungent observations intended to suggest and inspire some common ground of opinion and sentiment. Nobody was inclined to dispute his leadership, but everybody was prone to assert his own. It turned out that each regarded himself and wished to be regarded as a man with a mission, having a clear idea how things were not to be done. There were Civil Service Reform Protectionists and Civil Service Reform Free Traders. There were a few politicians, who were discovered to be spoilsmen, the unforgivable sin, and quickly dismissed as such.

Coherence was the missing ingredient. Not a man jack of them was willing to commit or bind himself to anything. Edward Atkinson pulled one way and William Dorsheimer exactly the opposite way. David A. Wells sought to get the two together; it was not possible. Sam Bowles shook his head in diplomatic warning. Horace White threw in a chunk or so of a rather agitating newspaper independency, and Halstead was in an inflamed state of jocosity to the more serious-minded.

It was nuts to the Washington Correspondents — story writers and satirists who were there to make the most out of an occasion in which the bizarre was much in excess of the conventional — with George Alfred Townsend and Donn Piatt to set the pace. Hyde had come from St. Louis to keep especial tab on Grosvenor. Though rival editors facing our way, they had not been admitted to the Quadrilateral. McCullagh and Nixon arrived with the earliest from Chicago. The lesser lights of the guild were innumerable. One might have mistaken it for an annual meeting of the Associated Press.

V

The convention assembled. It was in Cincinnati's great Music Hall. Schurz presided. Who that was there will ever forget his opening words: "This is moving day." He was just turned forty-two; in his physiognomy a scholarly *Herr Doktor*; in his trim lithe figure a graceful athlete; in the tones of his voice an orator.

Even the bespectacled doctrinaires of the East, whence, since the days when the Star of Bethlehem shone over the desert, wisdom and wise men have had their emanation, were moved to something like enthusiasm. The rest of us were fervid and aglow. Two days and a night and a half the Quadrilateral had the world in a sling and things its own way. It had been agreed, as I have said, to limit the field to Adams, Trumbull and Greeley; Greeley being out of it, as having no chance, still further abridged it to Adams and Trumbull; and, Trumbull not developing very strong, Bowles, Halstead and I, even White, began to be sure of Adams on the first ballot; Adams the indifferent, who had sailed away for Europe, observing that he was not a candidate for the nomination and otherwise intimating his disdain of us and it.

Matters thus apparently cocked and primed, the convention adjourned over the first night of its session with everybody happy except the D. Davis contingent, which lingered on the scene, but knew its "cake was dough." If we had forced a vote that night, as we might have done, we should have nominated Adams. But inspired by the bravery of youth and inexperience we let the golden opportunity slip. The throng of delegates and the audience dispersed.

In those days, it being the business of my life to turn day into night and night into day, it was not my habit to seek my bed much before the presses began to thunder below, and this night proving no exception, and being tempted by a party of Kentuckians, who had come, some to back me and some to watch me, I did not quit their agreeable society until the "wee short hours ayont the twal." Before turning in I glanced at the early edition of the Commercial, to see that something—I was too tired to decipher precisely what— had happened. It was, in point of fact, the arrival about midnight of Gen. Frank P. Blair and Governor B. Gratz Brown.

I had in my possession documents that would have induced at least one of them to pause before making himself too conspicuous. The Quadrilateral, excepting Reid, knew this. We had separated upon the adjournment of the convention. I being across the river in Covington, their search was unavailing. I was not to be found. They were in despair. When having had a few hours of rest I reached the convention hall toward noon it was too late.

I got into the thick of it in time to see the close, not without an angry collision with that one of the newly arrived actors whose coming had changed the course of events, with whom I had lifelong relations of affectionate intimacy. Sailing but the other day through Mediterranean waters with Joseph Pulitzer, who, then a mere youth, was yet the secretary of the convention, he recalled the scene; the unexpected and not over attractive appearance of the governor of Missouri; his not very pleasing yet ingenious speech; the stoical, almost lethargic indifference of Schurz.

"Carl Schurz," said Pulitzer, "was the most industrious and the least energetic man I have ever worked with. A word from him at that crisis would have completely routed Blair and squelched Brown. It was simply not in him to speak it."

Greeley was nominated amid a whirl of enthusiasm, his workers, with Whitelaw Reid at their head, having maintained an admirable and effective organization and being thoroughly prepared to take advantage of the opportune moment. It was the logic of the event that B. Gratz Brown should be placed on the ticket with him.

The Quadrilateral was nowhere. It was done for. The impossible had come to pass. There rose thereafter a friendly issue of veracity between Schurz and myself, which illustrates our state of mind. My version is that we left the convention hall together with an immaterial train of after incidents, his that we had not met after the adjournment—he quite sure of this because he had looked for me in vain.

"Schurz was right," said Joseph Pulitzer upon the occasion of our yachting cruise just mentioned, "I know, for he and I went directly from the hall with Judge Stallo to his home on Walnut Hills, where we dined and passed the afternoon."

[Illustration: Mrs. Lincoln in 1861 *From a Photograph by M. B. Brady*]

The Quadrilateral had been knocked into a cocked hat. Whitelaw Reid was the only one of us who clearly understood the situation and thoroughly knew what he was about. He came to me and said: "I have won, and you people have lost. I shall expect that you stand by the agreement and meet me as my guests at dinner to-night. But if you do not personally look after this the others will not be there."

I was as badly hurt as any, but a bond is a bond and I did as he desired, succeeding partly by coaxing and partly by insisting, though it was devious work.

Frostier conviviality I have never sat down to than Reid's dinner. Horace White looked more than ever like an iceberg, Sam Bowles was diplomatic but ineffusive, Schurz was as a death's head at the board; Halstead and I through sheer bravado tried to enliven the feast. But they would none of us, nor it, and we separated early and sadly, reformers hoist by their own petard.

VI

The reception by the country of the nomination of Horace Greeley was as inexplicable to the politicians as the nomination itself had been unexpected by the Quadrilateral. The people rose to it. The sentimental, the fantastic and the paradoxical in human nature had to do with this. At the South an ebullition of pleased surprise grew into positive enthusiasm. Peace was the need if not the longing of the Southern heart, and Greeley's had been the first hand stretched out to the South from the enemy's camp—very bravely, too, for he had signed the bail bond of Jefferson Davis—and quick upon the news flashed the response from generous men eager for the chance to pay something upon a recognized debt of gratitude.

Except for this spontaneous uprising, which continued unabated in July, the Democratic Party could not have been induced at Baltimore to ratify the proceedings at Cincinnati and formally to make Greeley its candidate. The leaders dared not resist it. Some of them halted, a few held out, but by midsummer the great body of them came to the front to head the procession.

He was a queer old man; a very medley of contradictions; shrewd and simple; credulous and penetrating; a master penman of the school of Swift and Cobbett; even in his odd picturesque personality whimsically attractive; a man to be reckoned with where he chose to put his powers forth, as Seward learned to his cost.

What he would have done with the Presidency had he reached it is not easy to say or surmise. He was altogether unsuited for official life, for which nevertheless he had a passion. But he was not so readily deceived in men or misled in measures as he seemed and as most people thought him.

His convictions were emotional, his philosophy was experimental; but there was a certain method in their application to public affairs. He gave bountifully of his affection and his confidence to the few who enjoyed his familiar friendship—accessible and sympathetic though not indiscriminating to those who appealed to his impressionable sensibilities and sought his help. He had been a good party man and was by nature and temperament a partisan.

To him place was not a badge of servitude; it was a decoration—preferment, promotion, popular recognition. He had always yearned for office as the legitimate destination of public life and the honorable award of party service. During the greater part of his career the conditions of journalism had been rather squalid and servile. He was really great as a journalist. He was truly and highly fit for nothing else, but seeing less deserving and less capable men about him advanced from one post of distinction to another he wondered why his turn proved so tardy in coming, and when it would come. It did come with a rush. What more natural than that he should believe it real instead of the empty pageant of a vision?

It had taken me but a day and a night to pull myself together after the first shock and surprise and to plunge into the swim to help fetch the waterlogged factions ashore. This was clearly indispensable to forcing the Democratic organization to come to the rescue of what would have been otherwise but a derelict upon a stormy sea. Schurz was deeply disgruntled. Before he could be appeased a bridge, found in what was called the Fifth Avenue Hotel Conference, had to be constructed in order to carry him across the stream which flowed between his disappointed hopes and aims and what appeared to him an illogical and repulsive alternative. He had taken to his tent and sulked like another Achilles. He was harder to deal with than any of the Democratic file leaders, but he finally yielded and did splendid work in the campaign.

His was a stubborn spirit not readily adjustable. He was a nobly gifted man, but from first to last an alien in an alien land. He once said to me, "If I should live a thousand years they would still call me a Dutchman." No man of his time spoke so well or wrote to better purpose. He was equally skillful in debate, an overmatch for Conkling and Morton, whom—especially in the French arms matter—he completely dominated and outshone. As sincere and unselfish, as patriotic and as courageous as any of his contemporaries, he could never attain the full measure of the popular heart and confidence, albeit reaching its understanding directly and surely; within himself a man of sentiment who was not the cause of sentiment in others. He knew this and felt it.

The Nast cartoons, which as to Greeley and Sumner were unsparing in the last degree, whilst treating Schurz with a kind of considerate qualifying humor, nevertheless greatly offended him. I do not think Greeley minded them much if at all. They were very effective; notably the "Pirate Ship," which represented Greeley leaning over the taffrail of a vessel carrying the Stars and Stripes and waving his handkerchief at the man-of-war Uncle Sam in the distance, the political leaders of the Confederacy dressed in true corsair costume crouched below ready to spring. Nothing did more to sectionalize Northern opinion and fire the Northern heart, and to lash the fury of the rank and file of those who were urged to vote as they had shot and who had hoisted above them the Bloody Shirt for a banner. The first half of the canvass the bulge was with Greeley; the second half began in eclipse, to end in something very like collapse.

The old man seized his flag and set out upon his own account for a tour of the country. Right well he bore himself. If speech-making ever does any good toward the shaping of results Greeley's speeches surely should have elected him. They were marvels of impromptu oratory, mostly homely and touching appeals to the better sense and the magnanimity of a people not ripe or ready for generous impressions; convincing in their simplicity and integrity; unanswerable from any standpoint of sagacious statesmanship or true patriotism if the North had been in any mood to listen and to reason.

I met him at Cincinnati and acted as his escort to Louisville and thence to Indianapolis, where others were waiting to take him in charge. He was in a state of querulous excitement. Before the vast and noisy audiences which we faced he stood apparently pleased and composed, delivering his words as he might have dictated them to a stenographer. As soon as we were alone he would break out into a kind of lamentation, punctuated by occasional bursts of objurgation. He especially distrusted the Quadrilateral, making an exception in my case, as well he might, because however his nomination had jarred my judgment I had a real affection for him, dating back to the years immediately preceding the war when I was wont to encounter him in the reporters' galleries at Washington, which he preferred to using his floor privilege as an ex-member of Congress.

It was mid-October. We had heard from Maine; Indiana and Ohio had voted. He was for the first time realizing the hopeless nature of the contest. The South in irons and under military rule and martial law sure for Grant, there had never been any real chance. Now it was obvious that there was to be no compensating ground swell at the North. That he should pour forth his chagrin to one whom he knew so well and even regarded as one of his boys was inevitable. Much of what he said was founded on a basis of fact, some of it was mere suspicion and surmise, all of it came back to the main point that defeat stared us in the face. I was glad and yet loath to part with him. If ever a man needed a strong friendly hand and heart to lean upon he did during those dark days—the end in darkest night nearer than anyone could divine. He showed stronger mettle than had been allowed him: bore a manlier part than was commonly ascribed to the slovenly slipshod habiliments and the aspects in which benignancy and vacillation seemed to struggle for the ascendancy. Abroad the elements conspired against him. At home his wife lay ill, as it proved, unto death. The good gray head he still carried like a hero, but the worn and tender heart was beginning to break. Overwhelming defeat was followed by overwhelming affliction. He never quitted his dear one's beside until the last pulsebeat, and then he sank beneath the load of grief.

"The Tribune is gone and I am gone," he said, and spoke no more.

The death of Greeley fell upon the country with a sudden shock. It roused a universal sense of pity and sorrow and awe. All hearts were hushed. In an instant the bitterness of the campaign was forgotten, though the huzzas of the victors still rent the air. The President, his late antagonist, with his cabinet and the leading members of the two Houses of Congress, attended his funeral. As he lay in his coffin he was no longer the arch rebel, leading a combine of buccaneers and insurgents, which the Republican orators and newspapers had depicted him, but the brave old apostle of freedom who had done more than all others to make the issues upon which a militant and triumphant party had risen to power.

The multitude remembered only the old white hat and the sweet old baby face beneath it, heart of gold, and hand wielding the wizard pen; the incarnation of probity and kindness, of steadfast devotion to his duty as he saw it, and to the needs of the whole human family. A tragedy in truth it was; and yet as his body was lowered into its grave there rose above it, invisible, unnoted, a flower of matchless beauty — the flower of peace and love between the sections of the Union to which his life had been a sacrifice.

The crank convention had builded wiser than it knew. That the Democratic Party could ever have been brought to the support of Horace Greeley for President of the United States reads even now like a page out of a nonsense book. That his warmest support should have come from the South seems incredible and was a priceless fact. His martyrdom shortened the distance across the bloody chasm; his coffin very nearly filled it. The candidacy of Charles Francis Adams or of Lyman Trumbull meant a mathematical formula, with no solution of the problem and as certain defeat at the end of it. His candidacy threw a flood of light and warmth into the arena of deadly strife; it made a more equal and reasonable division of parties possible; it put the Southern half of the country in a position to plead its own case by showing the Northern half that it was not wholly recalcitrant or reactionary; and it made way for real issues of pith and moment relating to the time instead of pigments of bellicose passion and scraps of ante bellum controversy.

In a word Greeley did more by his death to complete the work of Lincoln than he could have done by a triumph at the polls and the term in the White House he so much desired. Though but sixty-one years of age, his race was run. Of him it may be truly written that he lived a life full of inspiration to his countrymen and died not in vain, "our later Franklin" fittingly inscribed upon his tomb.

Chapter the Twelfth

The Ideal in Public Life — Politicians, Statesmen and Philo-
sophers — The
Disputed Presidency in 1876 — The Personality and Character of
Mr.
Tilden — His Election and Exclusion by a Partisan Tribunal

I

The soul of journalism is disinterestedness. But neither as a principle nor an asset had this been generally discovered fifty years ago.
Most of my younger life I was accused of ulterior motives of political ambition, whereas I had seen too much of preferment not to
abhor it. To me, as to my father, office has seemed ever a badge of
servitude. For a long time, indeed, I nursed the delusions of the
ideal. The love of the ideal has not in my old age quite deserted me.
But I have seen the claim of it so much abused that when a public
man calls it for a witness I begin to suspect his sincerity.

A virile old friend of mine — who lived in Texas, though he went
there from Rhode Island — used to declare with sententious emphasis that war is the state of man. "Sir," he was wont to observe,
addressing me as if I were personally accountable, "you are emascu-
lating the human species. You are changing men into women and
women into men. You are teaching everybody to read, nobody to
think; and do you know where you will end, sir? Extermination,
sir — extermination! On the north side of the North Pole there is
another world peopled by giants; ten thousand millions at the very
least; every giant of them a hundred feet high. Now about the time
you have reduced your universe to complete effeminacy some fool
with a pick-axe will break through the thin partition — the mere ice

curtain—separating these giants from us, and then they will sweep through and swoop down and swallow you, sir, and the likes of you, with your topsy-turvy civilization, your boasted literature and science and art!"

This old friend of mine had a sure recipe for success in public life. "Whenever you get up to make a speech," said he, "begin by proclaiming yourself the purest, the most disinterested of living men, and end by intimating that you are the bravest;" and then with the charming inconsistency of the dreamer he would add: "If there be anything on this earth that I despise it is bluster."

Decidedly he was not a disciple of Ralph Waldo Emerson. Yet he, too, in his way was an idealist, and for all his oddity a man of intellectual integrity, a trifle exaggerated perhaps in its methods and illustrations, but true to his convictions of right and duty, as Emerson would have had him be. For was it not Emerson who exclaimed, "We will walk on our own feet; we will work with our own hands; we will speak our own minds?"

II

In spite of our good Woodrow and our lamented Theodore I have quite made up my mind that there is no such thing as the ideal in public life, construing public life to refer to political transactions. The ideal may exist in art and letters, and sometimes very young men imagine that it exists in very young women. But here we must draw the line. As society is constituted the ideal has no place, not even standing room, in the arena of civics.

If we would make a place for it we must begin by realizing this. The painter, like the lover, is a law unto himself, with his little picture—the poet, also, with his little rhyme—his atelier his universe, his attic his field of battle, his weapons the utensils of his craft—he himself his own Providence. It is not so in the world of action, where the conditions are directly reversed; where the one player contends against many players, seen and unseen; where each move is met by some counter-move; where the finest touches are often un-noted of men or rudely blotted out by a mysterious hand stretched forth from the darkness.

"I wish I could be as sure of anything," said Melbourne, "as Tom Macaulay is of everything." Melbourne was a man of affairs, Macaulay a man of books; and so throughout the story the men of action have been fatalists, from Cæsar to Napoleon and Bismarck, nothing certain except the invisible player behind the screen.

Of all human contrivances the most imperfect is government. In spite of the essays of Bentham and Mill the science of government has yet to be discovered. The ideal statesman can only exist in the ideal state, which has never existed.

The politician, like the poor, we have always with us. As long as men delegate to other men the function of acting for them, of thin-king for them, we shall continue to have him.

He is a variable quantity. In the crowded centers his distin-guishing marks are short hair and cunning; upon the frontier, sen-timent and the six-shooter! In New York he becomes a boss; in Ken-tucky and Texas, a fighter and an orator. But the statesman—the ideal statesman—in the mind's eye, Horatio! Bound by practical limitations such an anomaly would be a statesman minus a party, a statesman who never gets any votes or anywhere—a statesman perpetually out of a job. We have had some imitation ideal states-men who have been more or less successful in palming off their pinchbeck wares for the real; but looking backward over the history of the country we shall find the greatest among our public men—measuring greatness by real and useful service—to have been while they lived least regarded as idealists; for they were men of flesh and blood, who amid the rush of events and the calls to duty could not stop to paint pictures, to consider sensibilities, to put forth the deft hand where life and death hung upon the stroke of a bludgeon or the swinging of a club.

Washington was not an ideal statesman, nor Hamilton, nor Jeffer-son, nor Lincoln, though each of them conceived grandly and exe-cuted nobly. They loved truth for truth's sake, even as they loved their country. Yet no one of them ever quite attained his conception of it.

Truth indeed is ideal. But when we come to adapt and apply it, how many faces it shows us, what varying aspects, so that he is fortunate who is able to catch and hold a single fleeting expression. To bridle this and saddle it, and, as we say in Kentucky, to ride it a turn or two around the paddock or, still better, down the home-stretch of things accomplished, is another matter. The real states-man must often do as he can, not as he would; the ideal statesman existing only in the credulity of those simple souls who are capti-vated by appearances or deceived by professions.

The nearest approach to the ideal statesman I have known was most grossly stigmatized while he lived. I have Mr. Tilden in mind. If ever man pursued an ideal life he did. From youth to age he dwelt amid his fancies. He was truly a man of the world among men of letters and a man of letters among men of the world. A phi-losopher pure and simple—a lover of books, of pictures, of all things beautiful and elevating—he yet attained great riches, and being a doctrinaire and having a passion for affairs he was able to gratify the aspirations to eminence and the yearning to be of service to the State which had filled his heart.

He seemed a medley of contradiction. Without the artifices usual to the practical politician he gradually rose to be a power in his party; thence to become the leader of a vast following, his name a shibboleth to millions of his countrymen, who enthusiastically sup-ported him and who believed that he was elected Chief Magistrate of the United States. He was an idealist; he lost the White House because he was so, though represented while he lived by his ene-mies as a scheming spider weaving his web amid the coil of mystifi-cation in which he hid himself. For he was personally known to few in the city where he had made his abode; a great lawyer and jurist who rarely appeared in court; a great political leader to whom the hustings were mainly a stranger; a thinker, and yet a dreamer, who lived his own life a little apart, as a poet might; uncorrupting and incorruptible; least of all were his political companions moved by the loss of the presidency, which had seemed in his grasp. And finally he died—though a master of legal lore—to have his last will and testament successfully assailed.

Except as news venders the newspapers—especially newspaper workers—should give politics a wide berth. Certainly they should have no party politics. True to say, journalism and literature and politics are as wide apart as the poles. From Bolingbroke, the most splendid of the world's failures, to Thackeray, one of its greatest masters of letters—who happily did not get the chance he sought in parliamentary life to fall—both English history and American history are full of illustrations to this effect. Except in the comic opera of French politics the poet, the artist, invested with power, seems to lose his efficiency in the ratio of his genius; the literary gift, instead of aiding, actually antagonizing the aptitude for public business.

The statesman may not be fastidious. The poet, the artist, must be always so. If the party leader preserve his integrity—if he keep himself disinterested and clean—if his public influence be inspiring to his countrymen and his private influence obstructive of cheats and rogues among his adherents—he will have done well.

We have left behind us the gibbet and the stake. No further need of the Voltaires, the Rousseaus and the Diderots to declaim against kingcraft and priestcraft. We have done something more than mark time. We report progress. Yet despite the miracles of modern invention how far in the arts of government has the world traveled from darkness to light since the old tribal days, and what has it learned except to enlarge the area, to amplify and augment the agencies, to multiply and complicate the forms and processes of corruption? By corruption I mean the dishonest advantage of the few over the many.

The dreams of yesterday, we are told, become the realities of tomorrow. In these despites I am an optimist. Much truly there needs still to be learned, much to be unlearned. Advanced as we consider ourselves we are yet a long way from the most rudimentary perception of the civilization we are so fond of parading. The eternal verities—where shall we seek them? Little in religious affairs, less still in commercial affairs, hardly any at all in political affairs, that being right which represents each organism. Still we progress. The pulpit begins to turn from the sinister visage of theology and to teach the simple lessons of Christ and Him crucified. The press, which used to be omniscient, is now only indiscriminate—a clear gain, emitting by force of publicity, if not of shine, a kind of light through whose diverse rays and foggy luster we may now and then get a glimpse of truth.

III

The time is coming, if it has not already arrived, when among fair-minded and intelligent Americans there will not be two o-pinions touching the Hayes-Tilden contest for the presidency in 1876-77 — that both by the popular vote and a fair count of the elec-toral vote Tilden was elcted and Hayes was defeated; but the whole truth underlying the determinate incidents which led to the rejec-tion of Tilden and the seating of Hayes will never be known.

"All history is a lie," observed Sir Robert Walpole, the corruptio-nist, mindful of what was likely to be written about himself; and "What is history," asked Napoleon, the conqueror, "but a fable ag-reed upon?"

In the first administration of Mr. Cleveland there were present at a dinner table in Washington, the President being of the party, two leading Democrats and two leading Republicans who had sustained confidential relations to the principals and played important parts in the drama of the Disputed Succession. These latter had been long upon terms of personal intimacy. The occasion was informal and joyous, the good fellowship of the heartiest.

Inevitably the conversation drifted to the Electoral Commission, which had counted Tilden out and Hayes in, and of which each of the four had some story to tell. Beginning in banter with interchan-ges of badinage it presently fell into reminiscence, deepening as the interest of the listeners rose to what under different conditions might have been described as unguarded gayety if not imprudent garrulity. The little audience was rapt.

Finally Mr. Cleveland raised both hands and exclaimed, "What would the people of this country think if the roof could be lifted from this house and they could hear these men?" And then one of the four, a gentleman noted for his wealth both of money and humor, replied, "But the roof is not going to be lifted from this house, and if any one repeats what I have said I will denounce him as a liar."

Once in a while the world is startled by some revelation of the unknown which alters the estimate of a historic event or figure; but it is measurably true, as Metternich declares, that those who make history rarely have time to write it.

It is not my wish in recurring to the events of nearly five-and-forty years ago to invoke and awaken any of the passions of that time, nor my purpose to assail the character or motives of any of the leading actors. Most of them, including the principals, I knew well; to many of their secrets I was privy. As I was serving, in a sense, as Mr. Tilden's personal representative in the Lower House of the Forty-fourth Congress, and as a member of the joint Democratic Advisory or Steering Committee of the two Houses, all that passed came more or less, if not under my supervision, yet to my knowledge; and long ago I resolved that certain matters should remain a sealed book in my memory.

I make no issue of veracity with the living; the dead should be sacred. The contradictory promptings, not always crooked; the double constructions possible to men's actions; the intermingling of ambition and patriotism beneath the lash of party spirit; often wrong unconscious of itself; sometimes equivocation deceiving itself—in short, the tangled web of good and ill inseparable from great affairs of loss and gain made debatable ground for every step of the Hayes-Tilden proceeding.

I shall bear sure testimony to the integrity of Mr. Tilden. I directly know that the presidency was offered to him for a price, and that he refused it; and I indirectly know and believe that two other offers came to him, which also he declined. The accusation that he was willing to buy, and through the cipher dispatches and other ways tried to buy, rests upon appearance supporting mistaken surmise. Mr. Tilden knew nothing of the cipher dispatches until they appeared in the New York *Tribune*. Neither did Mr. George W. Smith, his private secretary, and later one of the trustees of his will.

It should be sufficient to say that so far as they involved No. 15 Gramercy Park they were the work solely of Colonel Pelton, acting on his own responsibility, and as Mr. Tilden's nephew exceeding his authority to act; that it later developed that during this period Colonel Pelton had not been in his perfect mind, but was at least semi-irresponsible; and that on two ocasions when the vote or votes sought seemed within reach Mr. Tilden interposed to forbid. Directly and personally I know this to be true.

The price, at least in patronage, which the Republicans actually paid for possession is of public record. Yet I not only do not question the integrity of Mr. Hayes, but I believe him and most of those immediately about him to have been high-minded men who thought they were doing for the best in a situation unparalleled and beset with perplexity. What they did tends to show that men will do for party and in concert what the same men never would be willing to do each on his own responsibility. In his "Life of Samuel J. Tilden," John Bigelow says:

"Why persons occupying the most exalted positions should have ventured to compromise their reputations by this deliberate consummation of a series of crimes which struck at the very foundations of the republic is a question which still puzzles many of all parties who have no charity for the crimes themselves. I have already referred to the terrors and desperation with which the prospect of Tilden's election inspired the great army of office-holders at the close of Grant's administration. That army, numerous and formidable as it was, was comparatively limited. There was a much larger and justly influential class who were apprehensive that the return of the Democratic party to power threatened a reactionary policy at Washington, to the undoing of some or all the important results of the war. These apprehensions were inflamed by the party press until they were confined to no class, but more or less pervaded all the Northern States. The Electoral Tribunal, consisting mainly of men appointed to their positions by Republican Presidents or elected from strong Republican States, felt the pressure of this feeling, and from motives compounded in more or less varying proportions of dread of the Democrats, personal ambition, zeal for their party and respect for their constituents, reached the conclusion that the exclusion of Tilden from the White House was an end which justified whatever means were necessary to accomplish it. They regarded it, like the emancipation of the slaves, as a war measure."

IV

The nomination of Horace Greeley in 1872 and the overwhelming defeat that followed left the Democratic party in an abyss of despair. The old Whig party, after the disaster that overtook it in 1852, had been not more demoralized. Yet in the general elections of 1874 the Democrats swept the country, carrying many Northern States and sending a great majority to the Forty-fourth Congress.

Reconstruction was breaking down of its very weight and rottenness. The panic of 1873 reacted against the party in power. Dissatisfaction with Grant, which had not sufficed two years before to displace him, was growing apace. Favoritism bred corruption and corruption grew more and more flagrant. Succeeding scandals cast their shadows before. Chickens of carpetbaggery let loose upon the South were coming home to roost at the North. There appeared everywhere a noticeable subsidence of the sectional spirit. Reform was needed alike in the State Governments and the National Government, and the cry for reform proved something other than an idle word. All things made for Democracy.

Yet there were many and serious handicaps. The light and leading of the historic Democratic party which had issued from the South were in obscurity and abeyance, while most of those surviving who had been distinguished in the party conduct and counsels were disabled by act of Congress. Of the few prominent Democrats left at the North many were tainted by what was called Copperheadism—sympathy with the Confederacy. To find a chieftain wholly free from this contamination, Democracy, having failed of success in presidential campaigns, not only with Greeley but with McClellan and Seymour, was turning to such Republicans as Chase, Field and Davis. At last heaven seemed to smile from the clouds upon the disordered ranks and to summon thence a man meeting the requirements of the time. This was Samuel Jones Tilden.

To his familiars Mr. Tilden was a dear old bachelor who lived in a fine old mansion in Gramercy Park. Though 60 years old he seemed in the prime of his manhood; a genial and overflowing scholar; a trained and earnest doctrinaire; a public-spirited, patriotic citizen, well known and highly esteemed, who had made fame and fortune at the bar and had always been interested in public affairs. He was a dreamer with a genius for business, a philosopher yet an organizer. He pursued the tenor of his life with measured tread.

His domestic fabric was disfigured by none of the isolation and squalor which so often attend the confirmed celibate. His home life was a model of order and decorum, his home as unchallenged as a bishopric, its hospitality, though select, profuse and untiring. An elder sister presided at his board, as simple, kindly and unostentatious, but as methodical as himself. He was a lover of books rather than music and art, but also of horses and dogs and out-of-door activity.

He was fond of young people, particularly of young girls; he drew them about him, and was a veritable Sir Roger de Coverley in his gallantries toward them and his zeal in amusing them and making them happy. His tastes were frugal and their indulgence was sparing. He took his wine not plenteously, though he enjoyed it—especially his "blue seal" while it lasted—and sipped his whisky-and-water on occasion with a pleased composure redolent of discursive talk, of which, when he cared to lead the conversation, he was a master. He had early come into a great legal practice and held a commanding professional position. His judgment was believed to be infallible; and it is certain that after 1871 he rarely appeared in the courts of law except as counsellor, settling in chambers most of the cases that came to him.

It was such a man whom, in 1874, the Democrats nominated for Governor of New York. To say truth, it was not thought by those making the nomination that he had any chance to win. He was himself so much better advised that months ahead he prefigured very near the exact vote. The afternoon of the day of election one of the group of friends, who even thus early had the Presidency in mind, found him in his library confident and calm.

"What majority will you have?" he asked cheerily.

"Any," replied the friend sententiously.

"How about fifteen thousand?"

"Quite enough."

"Twenty-five thousand?"

"Still better."

"The majority," he said, "will be a little in excess of fifty thousand."

It was 53,315. His estimate was not guesswork. He had organized his campaign by school districts. His canvass system was perfect, his canvassers were as penetrating and careful as census takers. He had before him reports from every voting precinct in the State. They were corroborated by the official returns. He had defeated Gen. John A. Dix, thought to be invincible by a majority very nearly the same as that by which Governor Dix had been elected two years before.

V

The time and the man had met. Though Mr. Tilden had not before held executive office he was ripe and ready for the work. His experience in the pursuit and overthrow of the Tweed Ring in New York, the great metropolis, had prepared and fitted him to deal with the Canal Ring at Albany, the State capital. Administrative reform was now uppermost in the public mind, and here in the Empire State of the Union had come to the head of affairs a Chief Magistrate at once exact and exacting, deeply versed not only in legal lore but in a knowledge of the methods by which political power was being turned to private profit and of the men—Democrats as well as Republicans—who were preying upon the substance of the people.

The story of the two years that followed relates to investigations that investigated, to prosecutions that convicted, to the overhauling of popular censorship, to reduced estimates and lower taxes.

The campaign for the Presidential nomination began as early as the autumn of 1875. The Southern end of it was easy enough. A committee of Southerners residing in New York was formed. Never a leading Southern man came to town who was not "seen." If of enough importance he was taken to No. 15 Gramercy Park. Mr. Tilden measured to the Southern standard of the gentleman in politics. He impressed the disfranchised Southern leaders as a statesman of the old order and altogether after their own ideas of what a President ought to be.

The South came to St. Louis, the seat of the National Convention, represented by its foremost citizens, and almost a unit for the Governor of New York. The main opposition sprang from Tammany Hall, of which John Kelly was then the chief. Its very extravagance proved an advantage to Tilden.

Two days before the meeting of the convention I sent this message to Mr. Tilden: "Tell Blackstone" — his favorite riding horse — "that he wins in a walk."

The anti-Tilden men put up the Hon. S.S. — "Sunset" — Cox for temporary chairman. It was a clever move. Mr. Cox, though sure for Tammany, was popular everywhere and especially at the South. His backers thought that with him they could count a majority of the National Committee.

The night before the assembling Mr. Tilden's two or three leading friends on the committee came to me and said: "We can elect you chairman over Cox, but no one else."

I demurred at once. "I don't know one rule of parliamentary law from another," I said.

"We will have the best parliamentarian on the continent right by you all the time," they said.

"I can't see to recognize a man on the floor of the convention," I said.

"We'll have a dozen men at hand to tell you," they replied. So it was arranged, and thus at the last moment I was chosen."

I had barely time to write the required keynote speech, but not enough to commit it to memory; nor sight to read it, even had I been willing to adopt that mode of delivery. It would not do to trust to extemporization. A friend, Col. J. Stoddard Johnston, who was familiar with my penmanship, came to the rescue. Concealing my manuscript behind his hat he lined the words out to me between the cheering, I having mastered a few opening sentences.

Luck was with me. It went with a bang—not, however, wholly without detection. The Indianans, devoted to Hendricks, were very wroth.

"See that fat man behind the hat telling him what to say," said one to his neighbor, who answered, "Yes, and wrote it for him, too, I'll be bound!"

One might as well attempt to drive six horses by proxy as preside over a national convention by hearsay. I lost my parliamentarian at once. I just made my parliamentary law as we went. Never before or since did any deliberate body proceed under manual so startling and original. But I delivered each ruling with a resonance—it were better called an impudence—which had an air of authority. There was a good deal of quiet laughter on the floor among the knowing ones, though I knew the mass was as ignorant as I was myself; but realizing that I meant to be just and was expediting business the convention soon warmed to me, and feeling this I began to be perfectly at home. I never had a better day's sport in all my life.

One incident was particularly amusing. Much against my will and over my protest I was brought to promise that Miss Phoebe Couzins, who bore a Woman's Rights Memorial, should at some opportune moment be given the floor to present it. I foresaw what a row it was bound to occasion.

Toward noon, when there was a lull in the proceedings, I said with an emphasis meant to carry conviction: "Gentlemen of the convention, Miss Phoebe Couzins, a representative of the Woman's Association of America, has a memorial from that body, and in the absence of other business the chair will now recognize her."

Instantly and from every part of the hall arose cries of "No!" These put some heart into me. Many a time as a schoolboy I had proudly declaimed the passage from John Home's tragedy, "My Name is Norval." Again I stood upon "the Grampian hills." The committee was escorting Miss Couzins down the aisle. When she came within the radius of my poor vision I saw that she was a beauty and dressed to kill.

That was reassurance. Gaining a little time while the hall fairly rocked with its thunder of negation I laid the gavel down and stepped to the edge of the platform and gave Miss Couzins my hand.

As she appeared above the throng there was a momentary "Ah!" and then a lull, broken by a single voice:

"Mister Chairman. I rise to a point of order."

Leading Miss Couzins to the front of the stage I took up the gavel and gave a gentle rap, saying: "The gentleman will take his seat."

"But, Mister Chairman, I rose to a point of order," he vociferated.

"The gentleman will take his seat instantly," I answered in a tone of one about to throw the gavel at his head. "No point of order is in order when a lady has the floor."

After that Miss Couzins received a positive ovation and having delivered her message retired in a blaze of glory.

VI

Mr. Tilden was nominated on the second ballot. The campaign that followed proved one of the most memorable in our history. When it came to an end the result showed on the face of the returns 196 in the Electoral College, eleven more than a majority; and in the popular vote 4,300,316, a majority of 264,300 for Tilden over Hayes.

How this came to be first contested and then complicated so as ultimately to be set aside has been minutely related by its authors. The newspapers, both Republican and Democratic, of November 8, 1876, the morning after the election, conceded an overwhelming victory for Tilden and Hendricks. There was, however, a single exception. The New York Times had gone to press with its first edition, leaving the result in doubt but inclining toward the success of the Democrats. In its later editions this tentative attitude was changed to the statement that Mr. Hayes lacked the vote of Florida — "claimed by the Republicans" — to be sure of the required votes in the Electoral College.

The story of this surprising discrepancy between midnight and daylight reads like a chapter of fiction.

After the early edition of the Times had gone to press certain members of the editorial staff were at supper, very much cast down by the returns, when a messenger brought a telegram from Senator Barnum, of Connecticut, financial head of the Democratic National Committee, asking for the Times' latest news from Oregon, Louisiana, Florida and South Carolina. But for that unlucky telegram Tilden would probably have been inaugurated President of the United States.

The Times people, intense Republican partisans, at once saw an opportunity. If Barnum did not know, why might not a doubt be raised? At once the editorial in the first edition was revised to take a decisive tone and declare the election of Hayes. One of the editorial council, Mr. John C. Reid, hurried to Republican headquarters in the Fifth Avenue Hotel, which he found deserted, the triumph of Tilden having long before sent everybody to bed. Mr. Reid then sought the room of Senator Zachariah Chandler, chairman of the National Republican Committee.

While upon this errand he encountered in the hotel corridor "a small man wearing an enormous pair of goggles, his hat drawn over his ears, a greatcoat with a heavy military cloak, and carrying a gripsack and newspaper in his hand. The newspaper was the New York Tribune," announcing the election of Tilden and the defeat of Hayes. The newcomer was Mr. William E. Chandler, even then a very prominent Republican politician, just arrived from New Hampshire and very much exasperated by what he had read.

Mr. Reid had another tale to tell. The two found Mr. Zachariah Chandler, who bade them leave him alone and do whatever they thought best. They did so, consumingly, sending telegrams to Columbia, Tallahassee and New Orleans, stating to each of the parties addressed that the result of the election depended upon his State. To these was appended the signature of Zachariah Chandler.

Later in the day Senator Chandler, advised of what had been set on foot and its possibilities, issued from National Republican headquarters this laconic message: "Hayes has 185 electoral votes and is elected."

Thus began and was put in motion the scheme to confuse the returns and make a disputed count of the vote.

VII

The day after the election I wired Mr. Tilden suggesting that as Governor of New York he propose to Mr. Hayes, the Governor of Ohio, that they unite upon a committee of eminent citizens, composed in equal numbers of the friends of each, who should proceed at once to Louisiana, which appeared to be the objective point of greatest moment to the already contested result. Pursuant to a telegraphic correspondence which followed, I left Louisville that night for New Orleans. I was joined en route by Mr. Lamar and General Walthal, of Mississippi, and together we arrived in the Crescent City Friday morning.

It has since transpired that the Republicans were promptly advised by the Western Union Telegraph Company of all that had passed over its wires, my dispatches to Mr. Tilden being read in Republican headquarters at least as soon as they reached Gramercy Park.

Mr. Tilden did not adopt the plan of a direct proposal to Mr. Hayes. Instead he chose a body of Democrats to go to the "seat of war." But before any of them had arrived General Grant, the actual President, anticipating what was about to happen, appointed a body of Republicans for the like purpose, and the advance guard of these appeared on the scene the following Monday.

Within a week the St. Charles Hotel might have been mistaken for a caravansary of the national capital. Among the Republicans were John Sherman, Stanley Matthews, Garfield, Evarts, Logan, Kelley, Stoughton, and many others. Among the Democrats, besides Lamar, Walthal and myself, came Lyman Trumbull, Samuel J. Randall, William R. Morrison, McDonald, of Indiana, and many others.

A certain degree of personal intimacy existed between the members of the two groups, and the "entente" was quite as unrestrained as might have existed between rival athletic teams. A Kentucky friend sent me a demijohn of what was represented as very old Bourbon, and I divided it with "our friends the enemy." New Orleans was new to most of the "visiting statesmen," and we attended the places of amusement, lived in the restaurants, and saw the sights as if we had been tourists in a foreign land and not partisans charged with the business of adjusting a Presidential election from implacable points of view.

My own relations were especially friendly with John Sherman and James A.
Garfield, a colleague on the Committee of Ways and Means, and with Stanley
Matthews, a near kinsman by marriage, who had stood as an elder brother to
me from my childhood.

Corruption was in the air. That the Returning Board was for sale and could be bought was the universal impression. Every day some one turned up with pretended authority and an offer to sell. Most of these were, of course, the merest adventurers. It was my own belief that the Returning Board was playing for the best price it could get from the Republicans and that the only effect of any offer to buy on our part would be to assist this scheme of blackmail.

The Returning Board consisted of two white men, Wells and Anderson; and two negroes, Kenner and Casanave. One and all they were without character. I was tempted through sheer curiosity to listen to a proposal which seemed to come direct from the board itself, the messenger being a well-known State Senator. As if he were proposing to dispose of a horse or a dog he stated his errand.

"You think you can deliver the goods?" said I.

"I am authorized to make the offer," he answered.

"And for how much?" I asked.

"Two hundred and fifty thousand dollars," he replied. "One hundred thousand each for Wells and Anderson, and twenty-five thousand apiece for the niggers."

To my mind it was a joke. "Senator," said I, "the terms are as cheap as dirt. I don't happen to have the amount about me at the moment, but I will communicate with my principal and see you later."

Having no thought of entertaining the proposal, I had forgotten the incident, when two or three days later my man met me in the lobby of the hotel and pressed for a definite reply. I then told him I had found that I possessed no authority to act and advised him to go elsewhere.

It is asserted that Wells and Anderson did agree to sell and were turned down by Mr. Hewitt; and, being refused their demands for cash by the Democrats, took their final pay, at least in patronage, from their own party.

VIII

I passed the Christmas week of 1876 in New York with Mr. Tilden. On Christmas day we dined alone. The outlook, on the whole, was cheering. With John Bigelow and Manton Marble, Mr. Tilden had been busily engaged compiling the data for a constitutional battle to be fought by the Democrats in Congress, maintaining the right of the House of Representatives to concurrent jurisdiction with the Senate in the counting of the electoral vote, pursuant to an unbroken line of precedents established by that method of proceeding in every presidential election between 1793 and 1872.

There was very great perplexity in the public mind. Both parties appeared to be at sea. The dispute between the Democratic House and the Republican Senate made for thick weather. Contests of the vote of three States—Louisiana, South Carolina and Florida, not to mention single votes in Oregon and Vermont—which presently began to blow a gale, had already spread menacing clouds across the political sky. Except Mr. Tilden, the wisest among the leaders knew not precisely what to do.

From New Orleans, on the Saturday night succeeding the presidential election, I had telegraphed to Mr. Tilden detailing the exact conditions there and urging active and immediate agitation. The chance had been lost. I thought then and I still think that the conspiracy of a few men to use the corrupt returning boards of Louisiana, South Carolina and Florida to upset the election and make confusion in Congress might by prompt exposure and popular appeal have been thwarted. Be this as it may, my spirit was depressed and my confidence discouraged by the intense quietude on our side, for I was sure that beneath the surface the Republicans, with resolute determination and multiplied resources, were as busy as bees.

Mr. Robert M. McLane, later Governor of Maryland and later still Minister to France—a man of rare ability and large experience, who had served in Congress and in diplomacy, and was an old friend of Mr. Tilden—had been at a Gramercy Park conference when my New Orleans report arrived, and had then and there urged the agitation recommended by me. He was now again in New York. When a lad he had been in England with his father, Lewis McLane, then American Minister to the Court of St. James, during the excitement over the Reform Bill of 1832. He had witnessed the popular demonstrations and had been impressed by the direct force of public opinion upon law-making and law-makers. An analogous situation had arrived in America. The Republican Senate was as the Tory House of Lords. We must organize a movement such as had been so effectual in England. Obviously something was going amiss with us and something had to be done.

It was agreed that I should return to Washington and make a speech "feeling the pulse" of the country, with the suggestion that in the National Capital should assemble "a mass convention of at least

100,000 peaceful citizens," exercising "the freeman's right of petiti-on."

The idea was one of many proposals of a more drastic kind and was the merest venture. I myself had no great faith in it. But I prepared the speech, and after much reading and revising, it was held by Mr. Tilden and Mr. McLane to cover the case and meet the purpose, Mr. Tilden writing Mr. Randall, Speaker of the House of Representatives, a letter, carried to Washington by Mr. McLane, instructing him what to do in the event that the popular response should prove favorable.

Alack the day! The Democrats were equal to nothing affirmative. The Republicans were united and resolute. I delivered the speech, not in the House, as had been intended, but at a public meeting which seemed opportune. The Democrats at once set about denying the sinister and violent purpose ascribed to it by the Republicans, who, fully advised that it had emanated from Gramercy Park and came by authority, started a counter agitation of their own.

I became the target for every kind of ridicule and abuse. Nast drew a grotesque cartoon of me, distorting my suggestion for the assembling of 100,000 citizens, which was both offensive and libellous.

Being on friendly terms with the Harpers, I made my displeasure so resonant in Franklin Square—Nast himself having no personal ill will toward me —that a curious and pleasing opportunity which came to pass was taken to make amends. A son having been born to me, Harper's Weekly contained an atoning cartoon representing the child in its father's arms, and, above, the legend "10,000 sons from Kentucky alone." Some wag said that the son in question was "the only one of the 100,000 in arms who came when he was called."

For many years afterward I was pursued by this unlucky speech, or rather by the misinterpretation given to it alike by friend and foe. Nast's first cartoon was accepted as a faithful portrait, and I was accordingly satirized and stigmatized, though no thought of violence ever had entered my mind, and in the final proceedings I had voted for the Electoral Commission Bill and faithfully stood by its decisions. Joseph Pulitzer, who immediately followed me on the occasion named, declared that he wanted my "one hundred thousand" to come fully armed and ready for business; yet he never was taken to task or reminded of his temerity.

IX

The Electoral Commission Bill was considered with great secrecy by the joint committees of the House and Senate. Its terms were in direct contravention of Mr. Tilden's plan. This was simplicity itself. He was for asserting by formal resolution the conclusive right of the two Houses acting concurrently to count the electoral vote and determine what should be counted as electoral votes; and for denying, also by formal resolution, the pretension set up by the Republicans that the President of the Senate had lawful right to assume that function. He was for urging that issue in debate in both Houses and before the country. He thought that if the attempt should be made to usurp for the president of the Senate a power to make the count, and thus practically to control the Presidential election, the scheme would break down in process of execution.

Strange to say, Mr. Tilden was not consulted by the party leaders in Congress until the fourteenth of January, and then only by Mr. Hewitt, the extra constitutional features of the electoral-tribunal measure having already received the assent of Mr. Bayard and Mr. Thurman, the Democratic members of the Senate committee.

Standing by his original plan and answering Mr. Hewitt's statement that Mr. Bayard and Mr. Thurman were fully committed, Mr. Tilden said: "Is it not, then, rather late to consult me?"

To which Mr. Hewitt replied: "They do not consult you. They are public men, and have their own duties and responsibilities. I consult you."

In the course of the discussion with Mr. Hewitt which followed Mr. Tilden said: "If you go into conference with your adversary, and can't break off because you feel you must agree to something, you cannot negotiate—you are not fit to negotiate. You will be beaten upon every detail."

Replying to the apprehension of a collision of force between the parties Mr. Tilden thought it exaggerated, but said: "Why surrender now? You can always surrender. Why surrender before the battle for fear you may have to surrender after the battle?"

In short, Mr. Tilden condemned the proceeding as precipitate. It was a month before the time for the count, and he saw no reason why opportunity should not be given for consideration and consultation by all the representatives of the people. He treated the state of mind of Bayard and Thurman as a panic in which they were liable to act in haste and repent at leisure. He stood for publicity and wider discussion, distrusting a scheme to submit such vast interests to a small body sitting in the Capitol as likely to become the sport of intrigue and fraud.

Mr. Hewitt returned to Washington and without communicating to Mr. Tilden's immediate friends in the House his attitude and objection, united with Mr. Thurman and Mr. Bayard in completing the bill and reporting it to the Democratic Advisory Committee, as, by a caucus rule, had to be done with all measures relating to the great issue then before us. No intimation had preceded it. It fell like a bombshell upon the members of the committee.

In the debate that followed Mr. Bayard was very insistent, answering the objections at once offered by me, first aggressively and then angrily, going the length of saying, "If you do not accept this plan I shall wash my hands of the whole business, and you can go ahead and seat your President in your own way."

Mr. Randall, the Speaker, said nothing, but he was with me, as were a majority of my colleagues. It was Mr. Hunton, of Virginia, who poured oil on the troubled waters, and somewhat in doubt as to whether the changed situation had changed Mr. Tilden I yielded my better judgment, declaring it as my opinion that the plan would seat Hayes; and there being no other protestant the committee finally gave a reluctant assent.

In open session a majority of Democrats favored the bill. Many of them made it their own. They passed it. There was belief that Justice David Davis, who was expected to become a member of the commission, was sure for Tilden. If, under this surmise, he had been, the political complexion of "8 to 7" would have been reversed.

Elected to the United States Senate from Illinois, Judge Davis declined to serve, and Mr. Justice Bradley was chosen for the commission in his place.

The day after the inauguration of Hayes my kinsman, Stanley Matthews, said to me: "You people wanted Judge Davis. So did we. I tell you what I know, that Judge Davis was as safe for us as Judge Bradley. We preferred him because he carried more weight."

The subsequent career of Judge Davis in the Senate gave conclusive proof that this was true.

When the consideration of the disputed votes before the commission had proceeded far enough to demonstrate the likelihood that its final decision would be for Hayes a movement of obstruction and delay, a filibuster, was organized by about forty Democratic members of the House. It proved rather turbulent than effective. The South stood very nearly solid for carrying out the agreement in good faith.

Toward the close the filibuster received what appeared formidable reinforcement from the Louisiana delegation. This was in reality merely a bluff, intended to induce the Hayes people to make certain concessions touching their State government. It had the desired effect. Satisfactory assurances having been given, the count proceeded to the end—a very bitter end indeed for the Democrats.

The final conference between the Louisianans and the accredited representatives of Mr. Hayes was held at Wormley's Hotel and came to be called "the Wormley Conference." It was the subject of uncommon interest and heated controversy at the time and long afterward. Without knowing why or for what purpose, I was asked to be present by my colleague, Mr. Ellis, of Louisiana, and later in the day the same invitation came to me from the Republicans through Mr. Garfield. Something was said about my serving as a referee.

Just before the appointed hour Gen. M. C. Butler, of South Carolina, afterward so long a Senator in Congress, said to me: "This meeting is called to enable Louisiana to make terms with Hayes. South Carolina is as deeply concerned as Louisiana, but we have nobody to represent us in Congress and hence have not been invited. South

Carolina puts herself in your hands and expects you to secure for her whatever terms are given to Louisiana."

So of a sudden I found myself invested with responsibility equally as an agent and a referee.

It is hardly worth while repeating in detail all that passed at this Wormley Conference, made public long ago by Congressional investigation. When I entered the apartment of Mr. Evarts at Wormley's I found, besides Mr. Evarts, Mr. John Sherman, Mr. Garfield, Governor Dennison, and Mr. Stanley Matthews, of the Republicans; and Mr. Ellis, Mr. Levy, and Mr. Burke, Democrats of Louisiana. Substantially the terms had been agreed upon during the previous conferences—that is, the promise that if Hayes came in the troops should be withdrawn and the people of Louisiana be left free to set their house in order to suit themselves. The actual order withdrawing the troops was issued by President Grant two or three days later, just as he was going out of office.

"Now, gentlemen," said I, half in jest, "I am here to represent South Carolina; and if the terms given to Louisiana are not equally applied to
South Carolina I become a filibuster myself to-morrow morning."

There was some chaffing as to what right I had there and how I got in, when with great earnestness Governor Dennison, who had been the bearer of a letter from Mr. Hayes, which he had read to us, put his hand on my shoulder and said: "As a matter of course the Southern policy to which Mr. Hayes has here pledged himself embraces South Carolina as well as Louisiana."

Mr. Sherman, Mr. Garfield and Mr. Evarts concurred warmly in this, and immediately after we separated I communicated the fact to General Butler.

In the acrimonious discussion which subsequently sought to make "bargain, intrigue and corruption" of this Wormley Conference, and to involve certain Democratic members of the House who were nowise party to it but had sympathized with the purpose of Louisiana and South Carolina to obtain some measure of relief from intolerable local conditions, I never was questioned or assailed. No one doubted my fidelity to Mr. Tilden, who had been promptly advised of all that passed and who approved what I had done.

Though "conscripted," as it were, and rather a passive agent, I could see no wrong in the proceeding. I had spoken and voted in favor of the Electoral Tribunal Bill, and losing, had no thought of repudiating its conclusions. Hayes was already as good as seated. If the States of Louisiana and South Carolina could save their local autonomy out of the general wreck there seemed no good reason to forbid.

On the other hand, the Republican leaders were glad of an opportunity to make an end of the corrupt and tragic farce of Reconstruction; to unload their party of a dead weight which had been burdensome and was growing dangerous; mayhap to punish their Southern agents, who had demanded so much for doctoring the returns and making an exhibit in favor of Hayes.

X

Mr. Tilden accepted the result with equanimity.

"I was at his house," says John Bigelow, "when his exclusion was announced to him, and also on the fourth of March when Mr. Hayes was inaugurated, and it was impossible to remark any change in his manner, except perhaps that he was less absorbed than usual and more interested in current affairs."

His was an intensely serious mind; and he had come to regard the presidency as rather a burden to be borne — an opportunity for public usefulness — involving a life of constant toil and care, than as an occasion for personal exploitation and rejoicing.

How much of captivation the idea of the presidency may have had for him when he was first named for the office I cannot say, for he was as unexultant in the moment of victory as he was unsubdued in the hour of defeat; but it is certainly true that he gave no sign of disappointment to any of his friends.

He lived nearly ten years longer, at Greystone, in a noble homestead he had purchased for himself overlooking the Hudson River, the same ideal life of the scholar and gentleman that he had passed in Gramercy Park.

Looking back over these untoward and sometimes mystifying events, I have often asked myself: Was it possible, with the elements what they were, and he himself what he was, to seat Mr. Tilden in the office to which he had been elected? The missing ingredient in a character intellectually and morally great and a personality far from unimpressive, was the touch of the dramatic discoverable in most of the leaders of men; even in such leaders as William of Orange and Louis XI; as Cromwell and Washington.

There was nothing spectacular about Mr. Tilden. Not wanting the sense of humor, he seldom indulged it. In spite of his positiveness of opinion and amplitude of knowledge he was always courteous and deferential in debate. He had none of the audacious daring, let us say, of Mr. Elaine, the energetic self-assertion of Mr. Roosevelt. Either in his place would have carried all before him.

I repeat that he was never a subtle schemer — sitting behind the screen and pulling his wires — which his political and party enemies discovered him to be as soon as he began to get in the way of the machine and obstruct the march of the self-elect. His confidences were not effusive, nor their subjects numerous. His deliberation was unfailing and sometimes it carried the idea of indecision, not to say actual love of procrastination. But in my experience with him I found that he usually ended where he began, and it was nowise difficult for those whom he trusted to divine the bias of his mind where he thought it best to reserve its conclusions.

I do not think in any great affair he ever hesitated longer than the gravity of the case required of a prudent man or that he had a preference for delays or that he clung tenaciously to both horns of the dilemma, as his training and instinct might lead him to do, and did certainly expose him to the accusation of doing.

He was a philosopher and took the world as he found it. He rarely complained and never inveighed. He had a discriminating way of balancing men's good and bad qualities and of giving each the benefit of a generous accounting, and a just way of expecting no more of a man than it was in him to yield. As he got into deeper water his stature rose to its level, and from his exclusion from the presidency in 1877 to his renunciation of public affairs in 1884 and his death in 1886 his walks and ways might have been a study for all who would learn life's truest lessons and know the real sources of honor, happiness and fame.